Palgrave Studies in Creativity and Innovation in Organizations

Series Editor
Roni Reiter-Palmon
Department of Psychology
University of Nebraska
Omaha, NE, USA

This book series presents the latest research on creativity and innovation in the workplace, showcasing the unique contribution that psychology can contribute to workplace innovation studies both now and in the future. Addressing individual, team and organizational issues of innovation at work, books in this series offer insight from organizational and social psychology to cover topics with key applications to business and management, design, engineering and other applied domains. Encompassing a broad range of types of organization, it investigates the psychology of creativity and innovation in non-profit enterprises, entrepreneurship, small business, and research and development contexts, among many other domains.

The series brings together research in creativity and organizational innovation to investigate a range of key contemporary issues. Topics addressed include the relationship between creativity, innovation and organizational performance; measuring creativity in organizations; applications of creativity and innovation for top management and senior leadership; and the potentially negative consequences of innovation.

More information about this series at
http://www.palgrave.com/gp/series/16308

Melinda J. Rothouse

A Mindful Approach to Team Creativity and Collaboration in Organizations

Creating a Culture of Innovation

palgrave
macmillan

Melinda J. Rothouse
Psychology
Saybrook University
Austin, TX, USA

Palgrave Studies in Creativity and Innovation in Organizations
ISBN 978-3-030-47674-8 ISBN 978-3-030-47675-5 (eBook)
https://doi.org/10.1007/978-3-030-47675-5

Cover illustration: stilllifephotographer/gettyimages

This Palgrave Pivot imprint is published by the registered company Springer Nature Switzerland AG.
The registered company address is: Gewerbestrasse 11, 6330 Cham, Switzerland

Acknowledgments

With deep gratitude and appreciation to the many friends, peers, colleagues, teachers, mentors, and fellow travelers, living and deceased, who have accompanied me on every step of my academic, professional, and personal journey of mindfulness and creativity over many years. I would specifically like to thank my dissertation committee at Saybrook University, Dr. Terri Goslin-Jones, Dr. Steven Pritzker, and Dr. Ruth Richards—for their insight, patience, and unwavering belief in me and in this research. I am also deeply indebted to my colleagues Michelle Poole, Amy Wolfgang, Sharanya Rao, and the whole team at Coaching4Good as well as Jen Spencer and the team at Creative Executive. And to Dr. Karel Bouse, my cheerleader throughout the process and who graciously reviewed my working manuscript draft.

To my Saybrook peers who provided immeasurable intellectual, emotional, and spiritual support, Diana Rivera, PhD, and Richard Talley, PhD.

To my most beloved circle of soul friends and colleagues whose support helped made this project possible on a fundamental human level with their good humor, insight, and deep love: Ingrid Von Sydow, Klare Marzano, Michael Walker, Ryan Gamble, Jase Farrar, Kristin Scheel, Palmer and Lucas McLean, Carolyn Miles, Charlotte Gullick, Dreux Carpenter, John Best, and Eric Brown. And to my friends and colleagues in the Jungian community, Jo Todd, PhD, and Jennifer Selig, PhD, for helping to lend a depth psychological element to my work over the past few years.

To my family, for helping to shape me into who I am today, for making it possible for me to push beyond the horizons of my wildest dreams and aspirations, and for their often-bemused support of all my adventures, academic and otherwise: Patricia Rothouse, Lloyd and Shirley Rothouse, Elizabeth, and Greg Hall.

To my grandmothers, Jay Rothouse and Maxine Beach, who taught me the value of art and artistry, and whose loving presence follows me long after their passing.

To my dharma teachers and contemplative arts mentors, who showed me how to see with new eyes and to experience the magic and sacredness of every moment, Acharya Moh Hardin, Lynn Wolfe, Lance Brunner, Steven Saitzyk, Anne Saitzyk, Miriam Hall, John McQuade, and Jake Lorfing.

And to all those brave souls actively working to make the world and its institutions more compassionate, kind, just, and equitable. May this work be of benefit to all beings.

Finally, these acknowledgments would not be complete without a very deep bow to Grace Jackson, Beth Farrow, and Joanna O'Neill at Palgrave Macmillan for their belief in the substance of this book and in my ability to bring it to fruition as well as for their patience, constructive feedback, and kindness through and through.

Praise for *A Mindful Approach to Team Creativity and Collaboration in Organizations*

"The perfect book for leaders interested in integrating mindfulness and contemplative arts into the structure of their organizations. Dr. Rothouse's experience as a musician and long-time meditator gives her approach a deeply authentic quality that can inspire cohesion and collaboration in teams."

—Steven Pritzker, PhD, Co-editor-in-chief of *The Encyclopedia of Creativity*

"This book is an essential addition to the rapidly growing field of organizational creativity. With a focus on humanistic and experiential themes, and balancing theory and practice, it will be immensely valuable to scholars and organizational leaders alike, enabling leaders, coaches, and facilitators to build a culture of collaboration and innovation within their teams."

—Scott Barry Kaufman, PhD, Author of *Transcend: The New Science of Self-Actualization* and *Wired to Create: Unraveling the Mysteries of the Creative Mind* (with Carolyn Gregoire)

"Here, from leadership and creativity coach, scholar, teacher and consultant, Dr. Melinda Rothouse, is an engaging mix toward developing a fresh innovative, collaborative, and mindful organizational culture. From its solid rationale in theory and research to its five-level approach, linked to exercises in mindfulness and contemplative arts, is a route to new connection, creativity and life in your group or business."

—Ruth Richards, MD, PhD, *Saybrook University*, Author of *Everyday Creativity and the Healthy Mind: Dynamic New Paths for Self and Society* (winner of a Silver Nautilus Award)

"Melinda Rothouse embodies authenticity, creativity, artistry and innovation in everything she does. I have been fortunate to be a part of her journey for the last several years and have witnessed first-hand the transformative power of her expertise and the impact of her work with leaders as a participant, as an observer and as a colleague. I'm delighted that she's chosen to share her wisdom and practical development tools in this book as a timely gift to us all. As technology accelerates our world at an unsustainable pace, there is an urgent need for both traditional wisdom and basic practices that will help us to mindfully maintain connection to ourselves and others so that we continue to thrive as humans. This book beautifully answers this call and serves as a relevant and practical roadmap that we can all learn from. Whether you're an emerging leader looking to grow your impact or a development practitioner who is seeking innovative ways to inspire and bring out the best in others, you will find value in the theory, relatable stories and tools shared in this book."

—Michelle Poole, PCC, Executive Leadership Coach and Co-founder of *Coaching 4 Good*

"This impeccably researched and eloquently written book is a gem through and through. One facet worth highlighting is the exercises at the end of the chapters. Dr. Rothouse generously takes us through their context and purpose, offers very specific instructions for implementation, and suggests questions for discussion and debriefing. This makes the book particularly pragmatic for coaches, consultants, and group facilitators like me—I'll definitely utilize many of Melinda's offerings."

—Jennifer Leigh Selig, PhD, Creative, Educator, and Co-author of *Deep Creativity: Seven Ways to Spark Your Creative Spirit*

"This is a book for leaders and teams looking to expand their mindfulness and awareness along with creative ways to increase their collaboration and effectiveness. Packed with exercises for individuals and teams, it gives leaders the ability to apply new insights, awareness, and discoveries for greater impact in their organizations and the missions they employ."

—Jen Spencer, Executive + Business Coach and Founder/CEO of *The Creative Executive*

"*A Mindful Approach to Team Creativity and Collaboration in Organizations: Creating a Culture of Innovation* provides state-of-the-art practices to generate team creativity and innovation. The mindfulness and contemplative arts practices have been tested in organizational settings and substantiated by scholarly research. This exceptional guidebook offers invaluable creativity resources for coaches, leaders and teams."

—Terri Goslin-Jones, PhD, Workplace Psychologist and Creativity Studies Lead Faculty at *Saybrook University*

"Rothouse has done a wonderful and thorough favor for those deeply invested in mindful institutional and organizational change. She has taken teachings more commonly applied to intimate meditation practice environments and translated them with great skillfulness for professional and educational use. This book is accessible while remaining deeply profound and scholarly."

—Miriam Hall, Co-author of *Looking and Seeing* and *Heart of Photography*, co-director of *Nalanda Miksang Contemplative Photography*, and Director of *Herspiral Contemplative Arts*

"Dr. Rothouse is a visionary of creative process and organizational thinking. Her ability to weave both personal experience and relevant research in an easily accessible way make this work compelling, persuasive and sure to influence the field of organizational psychology for decades to come. Brava!"

—Diana Rivera, PhD, PCC, Psychologist and Founder of *Creative Empowerment Coaching*

"Dr. Rothouse has written a must-read book for anyone involved in any kind of organizational system, be it a corporation, non-profit, professional firm, or community group. This is a potentially paradigm-changing work that is dynamic, accessible and inspirational. It sparkles and hums with enthusiasm, common-sense, and potential for positive change."

—Karel James Bouse, PhD, Author of *Neo-shamanism and Mental Health*

Contents

About the Author

Melinda Rothouse, PhD, is a leadership, creativity, and career coach, consultant, educator, and facilitator based in Austin, Texas. She helps individuals and organizations tap into their innate creativity for greater insight, innovation, collaboration, and resilience. She is the founder of Austin Writing Coach and co-founder of Syncreate. She holds master's degrees in religious studies and performance studies, along with a PhD in psychology with a specialization in creativity studies from Saybrook University. Her dissertation research explored how mindfulness and contemplative arts may be used to facilitate creativity and collaboration among organizational teams. She is also a musician and photographer, and she leads workshops and retreats both in the US and internationally on mindfulness, creativity, and contemplative arts.

List of Figures

CHAPTER 1

Introduction

Abstract This book explores how mindfulness and contemplative arts practices can help to foster team creativity and collaboration in organizational settings. The introduction orients the reader to the subject of mindfulness and contemplative arts, and presents a five-level model of how mindfulness practices can support team creativity and collaboration which will be elaborated throughout the book. The introduction also describes the organization of the book, which presents relevant research into mindfulness and creativity in organizations, as well as practical, mindfulness-based exercises designed to foster creative collaboration among organizational teams.

Keywords Mindfulness • Contemplative arts • Team creativity • Collaboration • Organizational creativity

This book explores how mindfulness and contemplative arts practices can help to foster team creativity and collaboration in organizational settings. The research and practices presented here include the key findings from my doctoral research (Rothouse, 2018), which explored the relationship between mindfulness and creativity in organizations, focusing on how mindfulness and contemplative arts practices may be used to facilitate and

M. J. Rothouse, *A Mindful Approach to Team Creativity and Collaboration in Organizations*, Palgrave Studies in Creativity and Innovation in Organizations,
https://doi.org/10.1007/978-3-030-47675-5_1

develop team creativity and collaboration. This book also reviews new research that has emerged in this rapidly developing field over the last few years, presenting the most recent scholarship on mindfulness and creativity in organizations.

My doctoral research developed out of my personal journey as a mindfulness and contemplative arts practitioner and teacher as well as my professional work as a coach, consultant, and facilitator focusing on creativity, career development, and leadership for individuals and organizations. These experiences informed my studies into the psychology of creativity and inspired me to explore how mindfulness and contemplative arts practices could be used to stimulate creativity and collaboration in organizational settings.

This book also synthesizes what I have learned from my explorations of mindfulness, team creativity, and organizational leadership in working directly with leaders, teams, and individual contributors working in a range of contexts from small startups and non-profit organizations to state agencies and major corporations like Dropbox, Indeed, Apple, and Dell. My professional experience as a coach and consultant has given me a window into organizational functioning (and dysfunction) across a broad range of industries, including technology, marketing and advertising, accounting and finance, architecture and engineering, state and local government, the non-profit sector, and academia.

My Journey with Mindfulness and Contemplative Arts

I began practicing mindfulness meditation in 2004 while living in New Orleans, Louisiana, and working as an academic advisor and adjunct professor at Tulane University. I had studied Buddhism extensively from a historical and cultural perspective during my master's program in religious studies, but I had never developed a personal meditation practice up to that point. I initially began practicing meditation at the suggestion of a therapist to work with stress and anxiety. While I found it beneficial for my state of mind, it was also difficult to cultivate a regular sitting meditation practice on my own without additional support.

In August 2005, as I was preparing for the new academic year at Tulane, the winds of Hurricane Katrina blew through my world, along with thousands of others who lost their homes, their jobs, and even their lives.

Katrina was an incredibly traumatic event for so many people, and it forever changed the course of my life. After a period of uncertainty and confusion, I ended up in Austin, Texas, where I had to rebuild my life and my career essentially from scratch. After settling in Austin, I also went through the breakup of a long-term relationship, which left me feeling more uprooted and unsettled than ever. As a result, I began attending a local meditation center where I received the support and encouragement to cultivate a daily meditation practice, along with a community of like-minded souls who would become my sangha.

I started taking classes and weekend retreats focusing on meditation and mindfulness, including a series of courses on contemplative arts. As I will describe in more detail in the following chapter, the contemplative arts encompass a variety of practices rooted in the traditions of Asian Buddhism that foster a mindful approach to art and creativity. Traditional contemplative arts disciplines included calligraphy, landscape painting, the tea ceremony, and many other forms. As contemplative arts practices have developed over time, they now also include photography and many other artistic disciplines, with a primary focus on the creative process itself, and on the state of mind of the practitioner, rather than simply on the end product. In my own experience, I have found the contemplative arts process to be very liberating and enlivening, offering a fresh approach to creativity. For example, starting in junior high school, I trained as a classical singer, with years of operatic voice lessons and workshops, and later became a singer-songwriter. Yet by my mid-30s, my personal musical practice had begun to feel stale and somewhat forced, even obligatory. When I began taking contemplative arts classes, I rediscovered the joy of creativity, with permission to play, to not know, and to approach the creative process as children do, with a "beginner's mind," as Zen Buddhist teacher Shunryu Suzuki (1970/2007) called it.

The contemplative arts teachings, as taught by Tibetan-born Buddhist teacher Trungpa Rinpoche and his students, emphasized opening to the senses and appreciating the vividness of our everyday world, in all of its richness. The exercises I learned and practiced in my contemplative arts training helped me to see the ways my mind would habitually label, categorize, and judge my experience, and allowed me to open more and more to the direct experience of the phenomenal world. Meditation and mindfulness practice allowed me to settle my mind and open to the possibilities that exist in "Square One" (Trungpa, 1996/2008), the space of infinite possibilities represented by the blank page, the fresh canvas, or the uncarved block, as the Taoists refer to it. Experimenting with creativity in this way brought me a tremendous amount of joy and lent a fresh energy to my songwriting and performance practices.

I also began to study contemplative photography during this time, which helped bring the principles of contemplative arts alive for me in an even more tangible way. In contemplative photography, we use the camera to help sharpen our sense of vision, to really see what is around us in a new way, including ordinary objects, scenes, and things we might otherwise take for granted and not really "see." Contemplative photography is a meditative practice that requires slowing down and paying attention. The goal is not to take beautiful pictures, but to simply see what is before us and use the camera to convey what we see, including color, pattern, texture, light and shadow, form, and shape (Karr & Wood, 2011; McQuade & Hall, 2015). The photos may appear very abstract, conveying vivid hues, striking forms, or simply the unexpected beauty of everyday objects, whether natural or human-created. The result is often surprising and extremely powerful, as the following images may help to illustrate.

These images, born of my own contemplative arts practices, express something of the contemplative arts process as well as what can arise from this type of mindful approach to creativity. The first image, a photograph, includes the elements of color, light and shadow, and organic pattern, drawing the viewer's attention to the sensuous shape of the leaves, how their curved lines play off of each other, how the light shines through them, revealing pattern and contrast. I remember marveling at this play of light upon the leaves, such a mundane but marvelous display of mother nature only existing for a moment before the sun shifted (Fig. 1.1).

To this day it remains one of my favorite photographs, and I can recall exactly where it was taken (at Casa Werma, a retreat center in Patzcuaro, Mexico), the temperature and feeling of the air on that day, the quality of the light, and so on.

The second image, this time of human-created objects, may not be immediately recognizable upon initial viewing. In contemplative photography one of the aims is to fill the frame completely with the *flash of perception* (McQuade & Hall, 2015), or what was most vivid to the photographer in the moment of encounter, so that the same flash will be clear to the viewer. In this case, the frame is filled with shape and color, the vividness and shiny quality of the red, as well as the curved shapes of multiple objects stacked together, which happen to be kayaks, stacked alongside a boathouse in Austin, Texas (Fig. 1.2).

Fig. 1.1 Leaves. (Photo by Melinda Rothouse)

When I have shown this image in art shows and presentations, people often comment on how striking they find it, even if they can't identify or name exactly what they are seeing.

The third image is a photograph of a collaborative calligraphy piece I created with two other participants during a three-day contemplative arts workshop I attended in Los Angeles, led by Steven and Anne Saitzyk, two of my contemplative arts mentors. We began each day of the workshop with a period of sitting mindfulness meditation, and each exercise was introduced with a series of instructions helping to ground the participants in our present-moment experience and bringing our attention to the particular contemplative arts principle we would be exploring. Most of the exercises, including this one, were done in silence.

We created this piece without any prior planning or discussion of what we would be creating together. The instruction was for the first person to simply approach the blank page without any preconceptions or ideas of what they wanted to create and to simply dip the brush in the ink and make a mark on the page, synchronizing body and mind in that singular moment of creation. Then, the second person was to first observe the

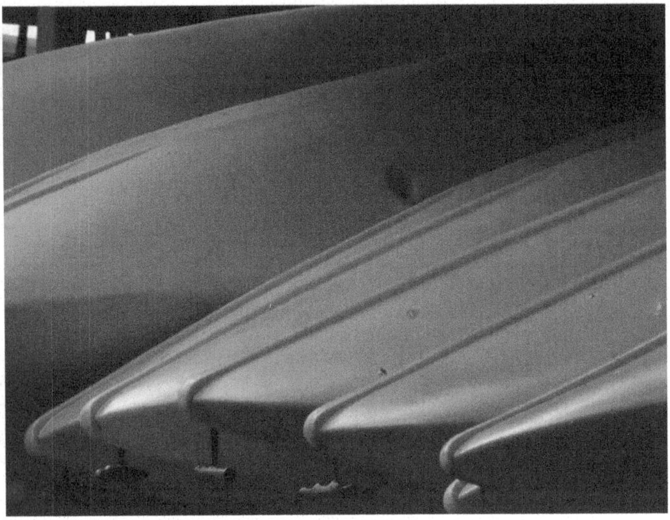

Fig. 1.2 Kayaks. (Photo by Melinda Rothouse)

mark that had been created, and then to dip the brush in ink and make a mark that in some way communicated with or related to the first brush stroke, again without planning or overthinking it. Finally, the third person, this time using red ink, was to observe the two strokes that had already been made, dip their brush, and simply make a third mark that somehow related further to the two existing marks, perhaps tying them together or playing upon them in some way (Fig. 1.3).

Although this piece was created spontaneously and collaboratively by three different artists without any prior communication, design, or intent, it hangs together as a coherent whole, demonstrating the creative potential of mindful collaboration.

A Mindful Approach to Creativity

Scholars exploring the connections between mindfulness and creativity have begun to use the term *mindful creativity* to signify a particularly meditative or contemplative approach to the creative process (Byrne, 2017; Capurso, Fabbro, & Crescentini, 2014; Dhiman, 2017; Langer, 2005). The actual experience of mindful creativity is beautifully expressed in a quote by Franz Kafka (1973), which conveys how the world comes

Fig. 1.3 Group calligraphy. (Photo by Melinda Rothouse)

alive when we slow down and start paying close attention: "It is not necessary that you leave the house. Remain at your table and listen. Do not even listen, only wait. Do not even wait, be wholly still and alone. The world will present itself to you for its unmasking, it can do no other, in ecstasy it will writhe at your feet" (p. 109). Once we begin to slow down and open our senses to the world, our creativity awakens naturally. Mindfulness and contemplative arts practitioners understand the mechanisms of this process, which I believe can be a powerful tool to support creativity and collaboration in organizational contexts.

Contemplative arts practice, a mindful approach to creativity, offers new possibilities for facilitating team creativity and collaboration in organizational settings. The contemplative arts have been introduced in the West mainly in the context of Buddhist meditation, within retreat centers and mindfulness workshops. However, this contemplative approach has many potential applications to the workplace and organizational settings to facilitate creativity and collaboration among teams, to shift organizational culture, and to support mindful leadership.

The exercises presented in the following chapters are inspired by a variety of teachings and practices I have received and experienced over the course of many years in different contexts and disciplines. These include my training and experience with mindfulness meditation, contemplative arts, improvisational theater, dance, and movement therapy. They also draw from my musical training in classical voice and opera, choir and musical theater, a cappella singing, and various group performance experiences. The exercises also draw from elements of my professional coach training and continuing education, including the Search Inside Yourself Leadership Institute Training (started at Google), Otto Scharmer's Theory U process, and many other professional development and continuing education trainings. When referencing specific exercises that have a known source or author, I attribute accordingly. Others I developed based on my own experiences working with teams and organizations in a variety of contexts, including leadership development, strategic planning and visioning, change management, and culture building.

I find, both for myself and for the individuals and organizations I work with, that when we take the time to slow down and practice mindfulness, we can open to a much broader range of possibilities than when we are hyper-focused on the immediate and urgent tasks of our daily work routines. This mindful approach allows us to look at the creative problems we are trying to solve from a wider perspective, while also allowing us to frame these problems in a more accurate way. It also affords us a sense of spaciousness and choice, rather than reactivity, which in turn yields a greater set of creative responses and solutions.

Team Creativity and Collaboration Model

My doctoral research employed a qualitative, action research paradigm, using arts-based and ethnographic methods, to explore the perceived effects of a contemplative arts workshop process on team creativity and collaboration within a functioning organization. The research findings demonstrated how a contemplative arts workshop process may be used to facilitate mindfulness, trust, communication, collaboration, and creative insights among teams and working groups. This book explores each of these themes in depth, weaving together contemporary psychological research on mindfulness and organizational creativity along with practical applications and contemplative arts exercises for scholars and practitioners.

The book is organized around five major themes that emerged from my doctoral research into the perceived effects of a mindfulness and contemplative arts workshop process on team creativity and collaboration, along with my professional work with teams and organizations. These themes include (1) Individual-Level Mindfulness; (2) Trust and Authentic Communication; (3) Team Cohesion and Collaboration; (4) Creative Ideation and Insights; and (5) Leadership: Creating a Culture of Innovation. The images below illustrate how these themes build upon one another to support team creativity and collaboration.

Following the principles of action research, my doctoral research study used qualitative, arts-based methods including a series of workshops, interviews, surveys, and ethnographic observation to investigate how the participants, designated as co-researchers, experienced the mindfulness and contemplative arts process. Action research generally follows a collaborative cycle of investigation that explores an issue or process of interest to a particular community of stakeholders and provides recommendations or solutions to improve the stakeholders' lives in some way. In this case, the co-researchers comprised six women who were members of a coaching firm based in Austin, Texas focusing on career and leadership development. I am also a member of this organization, which afforded me a unique opportunity, in keeping with the methods of action research, to conduct this collaborative study as both an insider and as a researcher in order to both investigate the effects of the contemplative arts workshop process on the team's collaboration and creativity, and also to help address some of the challenges and aspirations the organization was facing during a time of change and transition.

The study explored two main research questions: "(1) What are the perceived effects of a contemplative arts process on team creativity and collaboration within a small-to-mid-size organization? And (2) What are the perceived effects on team creativity and collaboration of working with a creativity coach/consultant?" (Rothouse, 2018). Data collection for this study included brief, semi-structured interviews and focus groups; researcher and co-researcher observations and field notes; qualitative written surveys; relevant organizational documents including company values statements; and creative products generated during the contemplative arts working sessions.

Each of these working sessions, which took place over the course of approximately six weeks, explored a particular theme related to mindfulness and creative collaboration using specific contemplative arts exercises. The sessions took the following format and order:

- Session #1: Mindfulness and Culture—Mindful Walk/Mindfulness of Environment and Collaborative Culture-Building Process
- Session #2: Opening to Experience—Direct Experience of Tasting
- Session #3: Somatic Awareness and Modes of Collaboration—Working with Movement and Gesture
- Session #4: Deep Listening and Structures of Collaboration

Once the working sessions and final debriefing session had been completed, I compiled, coded, analyzed, and interpreted using well-recognized qualitative and action research data analysis methods focusing on description, thematic analysis, and interpretation. The major themes that emerged regarding the perceived effects of the mindfulness and contemplative arts process on team creativity and collaboration included (1) Mindfulness: Relaxation, Openness, and Self-Awareness; (2) Trust and Authentic Communication; (3) Team Cohesion and Collaboration; and (4) Insights into the Creative Process (Rothouse, 2018).

The results further indicated a relationship between these four themes, such that each one in turn built upon and enhanced the others. Specifically, individual-level mindfulness laid the foundation for trust and communication among the group, which in turn supported team cohesion and collaboration, which then led to specific insights into the group's creative process. From these results I developed a model illustrating how a mindfulness and contemplative arts process can be used to support creativity and collaboration among teams and organizations. The following image provides a graphic overview of the research design and findings (Fig. 1.4):

This image illustrates how basic mindfulness practice, which supports individual-level relaxation, openness, and self-awareness, can pave the way for a deeper level of trust and communication within a team or group of collaborators. As trust and communication opens up, this in turn allows for a greater sense of connection, cohesion, and collaboration within a group, which can then lead to creative insights. This way of understanding group creativity and collaboration from the perspective of mindfulness has important implications:

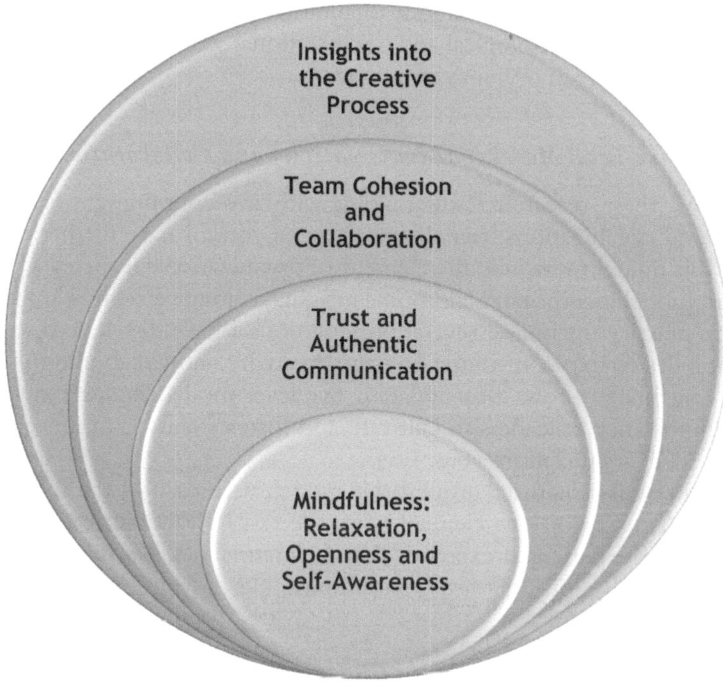

Fig. 1.4 Team creativity and collaboration model (Rothouse, 2018)

> These findings offer new insight into existing research on mindfulness and creativity by showing how mindfulness practices may be woven together with arts activities (in this case, contemplative arts) to support collaboration and creative thinking in organizations. The model described above suggests a suitable synergy for using mindfulness as a basis, together with arts activities, to enhance team collaboration and facilitate creative insights. Beginning with mindfulness as a foundational practice to support individual-level relaxation, openness, and self-awareness, facilitators can then employ arts activities to help build trust, authentic communication, and dialogue within a group. With this sense of openness and trust, group cohesion and collaboration can begin to coalesce, yielding creative insights. This particular combination of practices can foster positive team dynamics and deeper ways of knowing, which can, in turn, support positive organizational change. (Rothouse, 2018, pp. 155–156)

This research contributed a unique qualitative and experiential dimension to the emerging psychological and organizational scholarship on mindfulness and creativity in organizational settings.

Five-Level Model of Team Creativity and Collaboration

Based on these research results, along with my continuing work with teams and organizations over the past several years, I have further developed this model to include the element of organizational leadership. This revised model incorporates additional insights from my coaching and consulting practice, including several presentations I have developed exploring how leadership contributes to team creativity and collaboration. The following image shows this updated, five-level model, highlighting the vital importance of leaders to cultivate and foster a culture of innovation within their organizations (Fig. 1.5).

The book is structured around this model, with each of the following chapters focusing on one element of it, the research literature associated with it, and experiential exercises that facilitators can use to support it, beginning with individual-level mindfulness and moving up through the model to leadership.

Chapter Summary and Organization

The following chapters discuss each of the five components of team creativity and collaboration in more depth, first surveying contemporary psychological research relevant to each theme, and then offering practical applications and exercises that can be used in organizational contexts to support it.

Chapters 2 and 3 lay the theoretical groundwork and describe relevant research which contextualizes the subsequent chapters. Chapter 2 offers definitions for essential terms and concepts, including mindfulness, contemplative arts, and creativity, and describes how these concepts relate to organizational creativity and collaboration. Chapter 3 surveys existing research on mindfulness and creativity in organizational contexts, including the benefits and drawbacks of mindfulness practices for group creativity. This chapter also describes how leaders, consultants, and coaches are currently utilizing mindfulness and artistic practices to facilitate team creativity and collaboration.

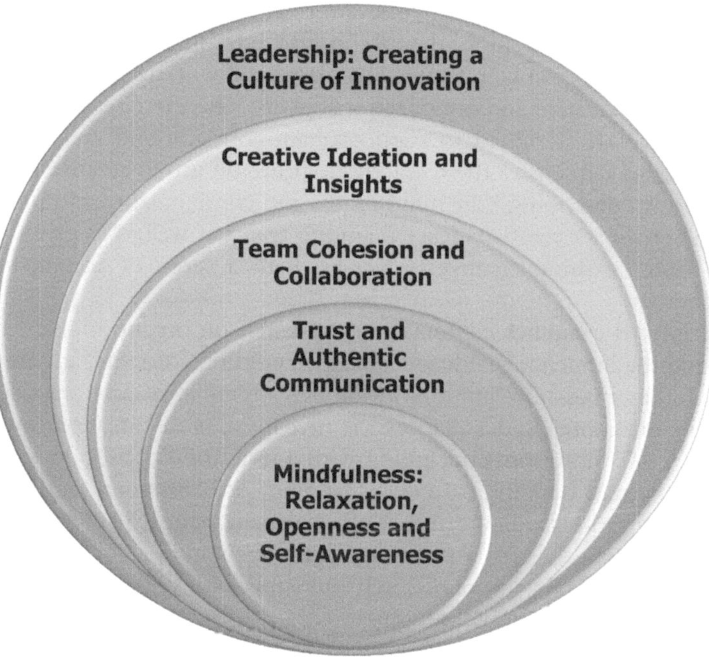

Fig. 1.5 Five-level model of team creativity and collaboration (Rothouse © 2019)

Chapters 4–8 guide the reader through the theoretical model for how mindfulness and contemplative arts practices support team creativity and collaboration. Each chapter first reviews relevant literature and research related to one of the levels of the model, and then offers specific exercises and activities that facilitators can use to help build the particular skills related to that level. Chapter 4 briefly surveys current research on individual-level mindfulness and its relevance to workplace creativity and then introduces a series of basic mindfulness exercises designed to support individual-level mindfulness among teams in organizations. Chapter 5 describes the importance of psychological safety, trust, and communication among organizational teams, demonstrating how mindfulness and contemplative arts practices can help to foster a sense of trust and open communication among team members. The chapter then offers a series of exercises designed to help foster trust and authentic communication among teams.

Chapter 6, in turn, discusses relevant research and scholarship on team cohesion and collaboration, describing how mindfulness and contemplative arts practices can help teams to coalesce and work together meaningfully toward creative and organizational goals. The exercises presented in this chapter are designed to support team cohesion and collaboration. Next, Chap. 7 discusses the research literature on group creative ideation and insight, describing how mindfulness and contemplative arts practices can help to spark creative ideation among teams as well as to give insight into teams' existing creative processes, with a series of accompanying exercises.

Chapter 8 examines contemporary research on organizational leadership and the influence that leaders have on culture, creativity, and innovation. It describes how mindfulness and contemplative arts practice can help organizational leaders harness creative insights and ideation to create a culture of innovation, concluding with a series of exercises designed to support culture building, strategic planning, and visioning, and to assist with organizational change and conflict management. Chapter 9 synthesizes key conclusions from this body of research and practice, describing potential avenues for future research and applications of this work in real-world organizational contexts.

Summary

This introductory chapter provided a brief overview and roadmap for the structure of the book, beginning with my own experiences with mindfulness and contemplative arts, which informed my doctoral research into how such practices can support team creativity and collaboration. It summarized the results of my doctoral research, which yielded a model for understanding how mindfulness and contemplative arts practices can be used in organizational settings to foster creativity, collaboration, and innovation. This model provides a structure around which the subsequent chapters are organized, beginning with Chap. 2, which defines important terms and concepts and their relevance to the major themes of the book.

References

Byrne, E. K. (2017). *Mindful creativity: An exploration of a mindfulness intervention on workgroup creativity* (Doctoral dissertation). Retrieved from ProQuest Dissertations and Theses (UMI No: 10271540).

Capurso, V., Fabbro, F., & Crescentini, C. (2014). Mindful creativity: The influence of mindfulness meditation on creative thinking. *Frontiers in Psychology, 4*. Article 1020. https://doi.org/10.3389/fpsyg.2013.01020

Dhiman, S. (2017). *Holistic leadership: A new paradigm for today's leaders*. New York, NY: Palgrave Macmillan.

Kafka, F. (1973). *Shorter works of Franz Kafka* (M. Paisley, Ed. and Trans.). London, UK: Secker & Warburg.

Karr, A., & Wood, M. (2011). *The practice of contemplative photography: Seeing the world with fresh eyes*. Boston, MA: Shambhala Publications.

Langer, E. (2005). *On becoming an artist—Reinventing yourself through mindful creativity*. New York, NY: Ballantine Books.

McQuade, J., & Hall, M. (2015). *Looking and seeing: Nalanda Miksang contemplative photography*. Madison, WI: Drala Publishing.

Rothouse, M. (2018). *Facilitating team creativity and collaboration using mindfulness and contemplative arts* (Doctoral dissertation). Retrieved from ProQuest Dissertations and Theses (Order No. 10823776).

Suzuki, S. (1970/2007). *Zen mind, beginner's mind*. Boston, MA: Weatherhill.

Trungpa, C. (1996/2008). *True perception: The path of dharma art*. Boston, MA: Shambhala Publications.

CHAPTER 2

Terms and Concepts: Mindfulness, Creativity, and Contemplative Arts

Abstract This chapter provides working definitions for the major terms and concepts that will be referenced through the book, specifically, *mindfulness*, *creativity*, and *contemplative arts*, and then discusses the relationships between them and their relevance to team creativity and collaboration. It describes how mindfulness practice can support openness to experience, cognitive flexibility, divergent thinking, and incubation, all important facets of creativity. It also characterizes contemplative arts practice as a mindful approach to creativity and discusses the importance of embodiment and somatic awareness in both mindfulness and creativity.

Keywords Mindfulness • Creativity • Contemplative arts • Openness to experience • Cognitive flexibility

Waking Up to the Sensual World

Before turning to academic definitions of the major themes to be discussed throughout this book, I'd like to share a little bit about how the practice of mindfulness and contemplative arts has informed my own approach to creativity, and to life in general. As difficult as it can be to convey in words, I want to share something of what it feels like to wake up to this moment and to the vividness and freshness of the phenomenal

M. J. Rothouse, *A Mindful Approach to Team Creativity and Collaboration in Organizations*, Palgrave Studies in Creativity and Innovation in Organizations,
https://doi.org/10.1007/978-3-030-47675-5_2

world, which is the primary gift that meditation and mindfulness practice has brought me.

As I began to practice meditation on a regular basis and to learn about contemplative arts, one of the most profound experiences I encountered was to be able to see in a new way. By slowing down my physical activity in sitting meditation and opening up to my senses, the world began to come alive to me more vividly. With an exercise as simple as turning slowly in a circle over the course of 10–20 minutes, I began to notice all of the little details of a room I had spent countless hours in, but had perhaps never truly "seen." Or by engaging in a contemplative photography exercise of simply photographing texture and pattern, filling the frame completely to the point of abstraction, I began to see and appreciate the characteristics and forms of everyday objects in a new way.

Once during a group meditation and contemplative arts retreat in Vermont with one of my mentors, music historian and mindfulness teacher Lance Brunner, we took a break from our daily sitting meditation practice for a silent mindfulness walk through the organic garden lovingly tended by the retreat center staff. To simply move though the garden in silence, single-file, at a slow, easeful pace, taking in the riot of color produced by lush red roses and stately purple delphiniums basking in the morning sun, to appreciate the tomatoes and greens that would later grace our dinner plates, along with the hum of the bees dutifully pollinating the flowers; it was all a delightful gift, making it impossible not to be grateful for the beauty and wonder of the natural world in all its simplicity and sophistication. I wondered why I didn't do this more often, on my own? Why did I need the structure of a meditation retreat and the instruction of a teacher to appreciate the moment and the world in this way? Alas, it is because I, like most people, spend my life busily rushing from one thing to the next, completing a daily to-do list, intent on meeting deadlines and obligations, fulfilling responsibilities and filling my senses with media, marketing slogans and images, and the latest headline, rather than taking intentional time for silent reflection and appreciation.

Several years later, I led a similar exercise of mindful walking while co-teaching a contemplative photography retreat in Patzcuaro, Mexico. I invited the participants to follow me in a silent walk through the lush gardens of the retreat center, to attend to the sights, the sounds, the smells, using all of their senses, without taking any photos at first, simply opening to the richness of the plants, trees, birds, fruits, and flowers surrounding us. I then asked them to find a spot on the ground and simply sit there, silently witnessing and observing, without taking any photos for 20–30 minutes, and only then to use the camera to record what they saw and experienced. Some of the resulting images were so vivid in their attention to detail—the curve of a leaf, a tiny insect perched on a flower petal, that these photographers might never have seen without first slowing down and paying such close attention to their surroundings, beyond the most immediate or obvious shot. My mantra for this retreat became "When in doubt, slow down." In this way, contemplative arts practice affords us the opportunity to come into accord with reality so that we can truly see, and thus work creatively with whatever is happening in the environment and in the moment.

Defining Terms

This chapter provides working definitions for the terms and concepts that will be referenced through the book, specifically, *mindfulness*, *creativity*, and *contemplative arts*, and then discusses their interrelationships and their relevance to team creativity and collaboration.

Mindfulness

The practice of *mindfulness* has gained tremendous popularity in the fields of psychology and medicine in recent years, drawing inspiration from Buddhist meditation traditions which emphasize present-moment awareness (Davis & Hayes, 2011). The practice of mindfulness (*sattipathana* in Sanskrit) is an ancient practice, dating back over 2600 years, to the earliest Buddhist teachings and scriptures from the Pali Canon (Analayo, 2003; Thera, 1994). According to traditional Buddhist teachings on the Four Foundations of Mindfulness, practitioners may train in mindfulness through sitting meditation practice, by sitting with legs crossed, becoming conscious of the breath, and observing their physical, bodily sensations along with mental and emotional states (Analayo, 2003; Koller & Koller, 1991).

Contemporary psychological and medical definitions of mindfulness, which have been adapted from the traditional Buddhist practice of mindfulness meditation, emphasize active awareness of oneself, one's internal states, and the environment. For example, Jon Kabat-Zinn (1991, 1994), who developed the widely known Mindfulness-Based Stress Reduction (MBSR) program, defined *mindfulness* as "paying attention in a particular way: on purpose, in the present moment, and nonjudgmentally" (Kabat-Zinn, 1994, p. 4).

As psychologist Dan Siegel (2007, 2010) observed, mindful states of consciousness include both the awareness of one's subjective experience, as well as a sense of openness and receptivity to whatever is occurring in one's field of perception and interpersonally on a moment-to-moment basis. Psychologist Ellen Langer (2014) took this one step further, defining *mindfulness* as "the process of actively noticing new things" (p. 68), which is also an important aspect of both contemplative arts practice and creativity more generally. In the context of Buddhist psychology, Jack Kornfield (2008) emphasized the relaxation of the body and mind as a pathway toward greater openness and equanimity.

My own understanding of mindfulness, based upon these scholarly definitions as well as my own direct experience of meditation and mindfulness practice, includes both the ability to focus attention and awareness on the present moment, along with an openness and receptivity to what is happening in the wider environment as perceived through the senses. This openness to sensory experience is an important element of contemplative arts practice as well, as discussed below.

Creativity

Researchers have traditionally defined *creativity* in relation to creative outcomes or solutions, with novelty and usefulness as the standard criteria by which creative products are judged (Plucker & Makel, 2010). This emphasis on creative products has historically led to a focus on the extraordinary masterworks of highly eminent artists, scientists, and innovators rather than on the creative process itself or the more experiential dimensions of creativity (Kozbelt, Beghetto & Runco, 2010). Creativity scholars refer to this type of creativity as eminent or "Big-C" creativity, as distinguished from more mundane creative efforts, or "little-c" creativity (Amabile, 1996; James & Drown, 2012; Kozbelt et al., 2010; Plucker & Makel, 2010). Kaufman and Beghetto (2009) introduced two additional types, "mini-c" (learning-related) and "Pro-c" (professional-level) with their Four C model of creativity. More recently, Gillam (2018) provided a valuable discussion of the historical development of such definitions of creativity, including both individual and socio-cultural approaches.

Following the development of humanistic psychology, with its emphasis on human flourishing and self-actualization (Maslow, 1962/2011;

May, 1975; Rogers, 1961), some scholars have embraced definitions of creativity as a fundamental human capacity, emphasizing the creative process itself, and on focusing on what creativity scholar Ruth Richards describes as *everyday creativity* (Richards, 2007, 2010, 2018). This more process-oriented understanding of creativity, based in humanistic principles, regards creativity as both a fundamental human capacity and an adaptive mechanism, which highlights the role of creativity in people's actual lived experience. As Richards explained in her book *Everyday Creativity and The Healthy Mind* (2018), this broader, more process-oriented view of creativity focuses on how we understand and make meaning of our experiences using our creativity rather than on the usefulness of particular creative products. This book draws inspiration from both views of creativity, with a deep appreciation of the meaning inherent to the creative process unto as well as the importance of usefulness and creative innovation in organizational contexts.

With respect to *organizational creativity* specifically, the notion of innovation becomes key, extending the traditional criteria of novelty and usefulness toward the production of innovative products and solutions (Mumford, Hester, & Robledo, 2012; Schwarz, 2015). The complexity of economic and social challenges that organizations must address in the twenty-first century requires an acute ability to find, define, and solve problems as well as to think creatively (Okuda, Runco, & Berger, 1991; Runco, 1994). To this end, Mumford et al. (2012) emphasized that creativity in organizational contexts involves "the production of high quality, original, and elegant solutions to problems…that are novel, complex, and ill-defined, in the sense that they can be construed and solved in multiple ways" (p. 4). This definition points toward the multifaceted nature of creativity in organizational settings.

In order to understand the complex dynamics of creativity at the organizational level, it is also helpful to utilize a *systems thinking* approach, which acknowledges the interconnections and dynamics of individuals interacting within a particular environment (Csikszentmihalyi, 1990, 1996/2013, 1999; Scharmer, 2009, 2013; Simonton, 2012). One of the great theorists of creativity and *flow*, the study of peak experiences, Mihaly Csikszentmihalyi (1996/2013) offered the following systems-oriented definition of creativity, which posits that:

> creativity results from the interaction of a system composed of three elements: a culture that contains symbolic rules, a person [or persons] who

> brings novelty into the symbolic domain, and a field of experts who recognize and validate the innovation. (p. 6)

This definition emphasizes that creativity does not happen in a vacuum, but rather within the context of a larger culture and system, and this is particularly relevant for organizational creativity. Indeed, as described by Marion (2012) this type of *collective creativity* "emerges from the interactions and conflicts of diverse people and ideas rather than from the mind of any given individual" (p. 458). The creative challenges that many organizations seek to address require cooperation and collaboration by a number of different players, both within a particular organizational system and with an understanding of the wider context in which the organization operates, such as the end user, client, customer, market, culture, political system, and so on.

Contemplative Arts

Contemplative arts practice also originated with Buddhist meditation traditions and can be understood as a type of moving meditation or off-the-cushion mindfulness practice. The defining feature of contemplative arts practice is its basis in mindfulness, or the particular state of mind of the practitioner. Indeed, according to The Center for Contemplative Mind in Society (2000–2015) *Contemplative Art* offers a way "to engage in the creative process with contemplative awareness" ("Contemplative Arts," para. 4). The emphasis here is on the creative process itself as much or more so than on the product or result.

With a basis in Buddhist meditation techniques and traditional Zen art forms, such as calligraphy, tea ceremony, landscape painting, and flower arranging, the contemplative arts in contemporary practice may include any type of artistic medium, such as visual art, music, photography, writing, and dance. These forms arose out of Chinese Taoism and Ch'an Buddhism, and found their ultimate flourishing in Japanese Zen Buddhism, with a minimalist aesthetic vision that honors the beauty and simplicity of nature in a very refined form. Traditional contemplative arts disciplines included calligraphy, landscape painting, and gardening, as well as the Japanese tea ceremony (*chado*), flower arranging (*ikebana*), and Zen archery (*kyudo*) (Chesshire, 2009; Daido Loori, 2004; Koren, 1994; Pritzker, 2011).

Contemplative arts practices were introduced in the West over the last century by a number of Buddhist teachers and their students who began teaching meditation, mindfulness, and contemplative practices in Europe and America, such as Japanese Zen teacher and founder of the San Francisco Zen Center, Suzuki Roshi (1970/2007), Tibetan Buddhist teacher and founder of Shambhala, Trungpa Rinpoche (1996/2008), and American Zen teacher and Abbot of Zen Mountain Monastery in Upstate New York, John Daido Loori (2004). Such practices offer an opportunity for practicing mindfulness not only on the meditation cushion, but also in the context of everyday activities and creative pursuits. With the more modern invention of the camera arose the practice of contemplative photography, which uses the camera as a tool to record the vividness of present-moment visual perception and awareness (Karr & Wood, 2011; McQuade & Hall, 2015; Zehr, 2005).

Until fairly recently, contemplative arts practice in Europe and the Americas has been associated primarily with Buddhist meditation traditions, with classes and workshops offered at retreat centers and mindfulness workshops. However, this contemplative approach has many potential applications within the workplace and organizational settings to facilitate creativity and collaboration among teams, to shift organizational culture, and to cultivate mindful organizational leadership. For the purposes of this book, the contemplative arts offer a bridge between meditation, mindfulness, and creativity that can be utilized to facilitate team collaboration and innovation. Contemplative arts practice thus offers a fresh approach to creativity that can be applied to a wide range of artistic mediums and creative settings. In organizations, contemplative arts practices can help individuals and teams cultivate presence and receptivity, thus opening the door to new creative possibilities.

A Deeper Dive into the Relationships Between Mindfulness, Creativity, and Contemplative Arts

Openness to Experience, Cognitive Flexibility, Divergent Thinking, and Incubation

So what exactly is the connection between mindfulness and creativity, and how do artistic practices, including the contemplative arts, fit into that picture? As we have seen, mindfulness involves the ability to be present to oneself, to others, and to the environment on a moment-to-moment basis. One of the hallmarks of mindfulness is a sense of openness to, and the ability or willingness to engage with, whatever is occurring in the present moment, which also turns out to be an important component of creativity.

With his theory of a person-centered psychology, Carl Rogers (1961) first introduced the concept of openness to experience, observing that "In a person who is open to experience each stimulus is freely relayed through the nervous system, without being distorted by any process of defensiveness" (Rogers, 1961, p. 353). Rogers explicitly connected openness to experience with creativity and the creative process, such that when one is open and receptive to one's experience as it is, creativity can arise and flow freely.

Over the years, many other creativity researchers have affirmed the connection and correlation between openness to experience, now commonly accepted as one of the "Big Five" personality traits, and creativity (Barner & Barner, 2012; Crescentini & Capurso, 2015; Kaufman, 2013; Kaufman et al., 2016; Kaviani & Hatami, 2016; Shi, Dai, & Lu, 2016; Silvia, Nusbaum, Berg, Martin, & O'Connor, 2009; Richards, 2007, 2010, 2018). People who score high in openness to experience tend to seek out and embrace new experiences; they are curious and also tend to show a high degree of imagination and creativity (Kaufman, 2013; Kaufman et al., 2016; Shi et al., 2016). My own research has investigated this deep connection between creativity and mindfulness with respect to openness and active engagement, particularly in organizational contexts (Rothouse, 2018).

In addition to openness to experience, creativity also involves *cognitive flexibility*, or the capacity to "switch between different concepts, to overcome fixed association patterns, and to make new associations" (Müller, Gerasimova, & Ritter, 2016, p. 278, following Guilford, 1967). From a psychological perspective, Siegel (2010) described how the practice of mindfulness can open the door to creativity:

> being receptive makes us available to shift into an open internal place and enable unpredictable states to be created so that we may resonate with others. This is a way of seeing how we can intentionally cultivate creativity and presence in our lives. (p. 13)

As these avenues of research illustrate, the qualities of mindfulness and creativity share many commonalities, including openness and receptivity as well as flexibility of thinking. While the traits of mindfulness and creativity share many commonalities, mindfulness practice can also help to support creativity by helping people to cultivate openness and a broader perspective from which to approach their creative processes.

Several researchers have specifically explored the connections between mindfulness and creativity, including the cognitive processes underlying both creativity and mindfulness, the mechanisms by which mindfulness can affect creativity, and at what particular stages of the creative process. In a chapter exploring the link between mindfulness and creativity in organizations, Kudesia (2015) described how creativity requires the reorganization of existing knowledge structures as well as a combination of divergent and convergent thinking, detailing how mindfulness supports both the processes of creative incubation and divergent thinking, which in turn supports a greater degree of cognitive flexibility, allowing individuals to open to new possibilities for solving creative problems rather than relying on past strategies or solutions.

Kudesia (2015) also described how mindfulness can support meta-awareness and working memory as well as attention regulation, along with indirect effects on stress-reduction and positive affect. Another recent study exploring the relationships between mindfulness and creativity affirmed the correlation between long-term mindfulness practice and divergent thinking (Berkovich-Ohana, Glicksohn, Ben-Soussan & Goldstein, 2017), while another found interesting connections between the psychological construct of mind wandering, mindfulness, and creativity, concluding that deliberate mind wandering coupled with mindfulness predicted both originality and creative achievement (Agnoli, Vanucci, Pelagatti & Corazza, 2018).

It is important to note that many different types of mindfulness and meditation techniques exist, some emphasizing focused attention and others cultivating open-attention, and that these techniques undoubtedly have different kinds of effects on creative ideation and output. In their book synthesizing contemporary neuroscience and psychology research on creativity, *Wired to Create*, Kaufman and Gregoire (2015) explored the link between mindfulness and creativity, focusing on the mindfulness-related benefits of improved focus, cognitive abilities, and observational skills that support creativity. However, they also warned that some mindfulness techniques can actually inhibit the kinds of defocused attention needed for imagination and creative thinking.

Specifically, Kaufman and Gregoire (2015) discussed the results of two studies investigating the effects of mindfulness training on creativity, which indicated that focused-attention meditation techniques can suppress imagination while open-attention meditation practices can facilitate divergent thinking and imagination (Baas, Nevicka, & Ten Velden, 2014; Colzato, Ozturk, & Hommel, 2012). Another recent study, however, concluded that focused-attention, or concentrative, meditation techniques can actually help increase cognitive flexibility (Müller et al., 2016).

A major figure in the academic conversation on mindfulness and creativity, including workplace creativity, is Ellen Langer (1989/2014, 2005, 2014). Her definition and approach to the study of mindfulness and creativity differs from those of other scholars because of its focus on mindful attention and information processing rather than on open awareness and receptivity, as discussed by Hyland, Lee, and Mills (2015). Kaufman and Gregoire (2015) described the significance of Langer's body of research, including that "she was among the first to show that exercising mindful awareness could lead to measurable improvements in cognitive function" (p. 104). Langer's research on mindfulness and workplace creativity will be discussed in more depth in the following chapter.

In a meta-analysis of 20 studies published over the last 40 years, Lebuda, Zabelina, and Karwowski (2016) found a weak but statistically significant correlation ($r = 0.22$) between mindfulness and creativity, with the strongest correlation between open-monitoring mindfulness techniques and a lower correlation between mindfulness techniques emphasizing awareness. The study also showed a stronger correlation between mindfulness and creativity measures focusing on insight rather than divergent thinking. They affirmed the results of prior research, positing not only a correlation but a cause-and-effect relationship between mindfulness and creativity, and suggested that mindfulness training can be a useful tool for increasing creative thinking and output.

It may be helpful to consider that different types of mindfulness practice can have different effects on the creative process, ranging from focused-attention techniques that help the mind to focus on the immediate tasks one is facing in the present moment, to open-attention techniques that support incubation, divergent thinking, and cognitive flexibility. Clearly this new and evolving field of research on the effects of mindfulness on creativity, and the question of which types of meditation techniques either support or hinder creative thinking, requires more research.

Mindful Creativity and Contemplative Arts

As described in the previous section of this chapter, meditation and mindfulness practices can help to foster the kinds of openness and active engagement required for creative thinking and problem solving. Similarly, contemplative arts practices extend the attentive presence of mindfulness into everyday creative activities (Daido Loori, 2004; Saitzyk, 2013; Trungpa, 1996/2008). As contemplative arts teacher and art professor Steven Saitzyk (2013) explained, in his book *Place Your Thoughts Here: Meditation for the Creative Mind*:

> Meditation helps synchronize mind with body, [align] right hemisphere of the brain with left, enhance intuitive and intellectual abilities, and promote clear perception. Much of art is about seeing and experiencing things as they truly are, and enjoying genuine spontaneity and unselfconscious, pure expression. Meditation helps us to better achieve this. It also dissolves creative blockages, reveals the source of creativity, and offers a path toward experiencing the sublime state in which our experience and knowledge merge into one. (p. 1)

Similarly, Zen teacher John Daido Loori (2004) emphasized how meditation and mindfulness practice help to quiet the mind and prepare the ground for creative openness to emerge: "The still point is at the heart of the creative process. In Zen, we access it through zazen [sitting meditation]" (p. 52).

In Episode 1 of Season 3 of the popular Netflix documentary series *Chef's Table*, there's a remarkable scene where the Korean Buddhist nun Jeong Kwan (the chef profiled in the episode) beautifully articulates the connection between mindfulness and creativity, framed in terms of the individual ego and the importance of transcending it:

> Creativity and ego cannot go together. If you free yourself from the comparing and jealous mind, your creativity opens up endlessly. Just as water springs from a fountain, creativity springs from every moment. You must not be your own obstacle. You must not be owned by the environment you are in. You must own the environment, the phenomenal world around you. You must be able to freely move in and out of your mind. This is being free. There is no way you can't open up your creativity. There is no ego to speak of. (Gelb, 2017)

This view of creativity as arising from presence and egolessness stands in stark contrast to traditional Western conceptions of art, which can be traced back to ancient Greek values of ideal beauty and perfection, as expressed in the symmetry and proportionality of classical Greek sculpture and architecture, and to the field of aesthetics, which emphasized concepts of pure beauty, pleasure, and the sublime (Janson, 1986; Sartwell, 2012; Slater, n.d.). In this view, art and creativity result from the careful application of skill, along with a "leap of the imagination" (Janson, 1986, p. 11) resulting from considerable mental activity and will.

Whereas the Western intellectual tradition has often regarded creativity as the purview of artists and scientists with extraordinary talent, emphasizing terms like, genius, virtuoso, originality, novelty, and uniqueness to distinguish artists and creative works from mundane craftsmanship, practitioners of contemplative arts understand creativity in a much more broad and inclusive way, as a universal human trait that is available to anyone and everyone who wishes to cultivate it. As Saitzyk (2013) explained, "creativity and the creative mind are not the exclusive province of those who choose to make art. The creative process takes place all the time in everyday life situations" (p. xiii).

From a Buddhist perspective, the significance of art stems not so much from the intrinsic value of a particular work of art, but from the artist's state of mind during the artistic process and the vividness or resonance of what is being communicated through a particular work of art. Natalie Goldberg (1986), the renowned writer, contemplative writing teacher, and Zen practitioner, has remarked in the context of writing practice, "Original details are very ordinary, except to the mind that sees their extraordinariness...We must remember that everything is ordinary and extraordinary. It is our minds that either open or close" (p. 75). Indeed, the tradition of Zen aesthetics brings the appreciation of ordinariness to full flowering with the concept of *wabi sabi*, which celebrates the beauty of imperfection in the humble details of life (Koren, 1994).

Mindfulness, Embodiment, and Creativity

Another important element of the link between mindfulness and creativity is the somatic experience of embodiment. As a growing number of psychology and neuroscience researchers are coming to understand, the physical body possesses incredible knowledge and wisdom, and yet the conscious mind is often only dimly aware of this immense somatic storehouse of information and potentiality. Indeed, the activities and awareness of the conscious mind represent only a tiny fraction of what occurs constantly in the body in the form of automatic physiological processes, incoming information from the sense perceptions, and non-conscious brain activities (Damasio, 1999, 2010; Fogel, 2009; Haidt, 2006). However, from the perspective of evolutionary psychology, Raskin (2012) has pointed out that embodied knowing, while often pre-verbal and thus largely unconscious, remains no less real or powerful than other, more conscious forms of knowing. This relates to creativity in that the body contains an incredible palette of information, memories, and experiences from which we may draw, if fully embodied, in our creative activities and endeavors.

Within the psychological literature, the term "embodiment" generally refers to how an individual experiences the physical body and sense perceptions in relation to conscious awareness. So often we think of the body as an object, somehow separate from the "self" or the mind, although many contemporary philosophers and psychologists, particularly those with a phenomenological orientation (as discussed in Varela, Thompson, & Rosch, 1991), have come to recognize the fundamental interconnection between mind and body, and the inherently somatic nature of experience and consciousness (Barratt, 2010; Damasio, 1999, 2010; Fogel, 2009; Gendlin, 1978; Merleau-Ponty, 1948/2004; Varela et al., 1991).

The contemporary psychological understanding of embodiment traces back to Merleau-Ponty's philosophical ruminations on perception and experience; his phenomenology of embodiment describes the relationship between the physical body, the act of perception, and the intimate, culturally dependent, dialectic relationship between perceiver and perceived (Dreyfus, 1996; Merleau-Ponty, 1948/2004, 1964). As Romanyshyn (2012) observed, Merleau-Ponty's philosophy of embodiment, as applied to psychology, "indicate[s] that meaning is an emergent property in human life" (p. 242). In other words, meaning arises out of the ongoing process of interacting with the world by means of the lived physical body within specific social and cultural contexts.

Somatic approaches to psychology, psychotherapy, and coaching understand the body and somatic or kinesthetic experience to be central to the process of psychological functioning, healing, and well-being. Emphasizing the deep interconnections between body and mind, Barratt (2010) defined somatic psychology as "the psychology of the body, the discipline that focuses on our living experience of embodiment as human beings and that recognizes this experience as the foundation and origination of all our experiential potential" (p. 21). At its heart, a somatically based psychology acknowledges the importance of physical and kinesthetic experience of psychological functioning, including the major roles that libido, sensuality, and life force play in human experience.

Eugene Gendlin's (1978) pioneering focusing technique helped to bring to the fields of psychology and psychotherapy an ever-greater appreciation of the body-mind connection, the role of affect and emotion in lived experience, and the importance of embodied knowledge and experience for healthy psychological functioning. With his focusing technique, Gendlin (1978) offered a specific tool for bringing the feelings and sensations of the physical body (the *felt sense*) more directly into conscious awareness (the *felt shift*). In her introduction to Gendlin's (1978) book *Focusing*, Marilyn Ferguson made explicit the connection between embodiment, awareness, and creativity:

> The felt shift is essentially identical to the freeing insight of the creative process. The spontaneously creative person has learned to pay attention to at first vague impressions that open into new meaning. Focusing improves scores on many measures of creativity…It helps to make the implicit explicit. It draws fuzzy, preverbal knowledge into definition and expression. (Gendlin, 1978, p. xviii)

From this perspective, the body is the ultimate source of all creativity.

Similarly, Rollo May (1975), in his humanistic treatise on creativity, *The Courage to Create*, explicitly addressed the connection between creativity and the physical body, noting "the inescapable unity of the body with the world. The body is always a part of the world" (p. 130). Subsequent generations of psychologists have further explored the connections between creativity and embodiment, notably in the context of flow experiences (Csikszentmihalyi, 1990, 1996/2013) and everyday creativity (Richards, 2007, 2010, 2018). In his studies of optimal experience, Csikszentmihalyi (1990) described a flow state as an experience in which "a person's body or mind is stretched to its limits in a voluntary effort to accomplish something difficult and worthwhile" (p. 3). The idea of flow is thus predicated on the experience of a person engaged in a particular physical or mental task, and Csikszentmihalyi (1990) particularly emphasized the embodied nature of the flow experience with respect to athletes and artists, in connection with physical practices such as dance, yoga, and meditation, and activities related to the sense perceptions, such as listening to music and eating.

These conceptions of creativity thus place a particular emphasis on the sense perceptions, the physical body, and the connection between creative acts and conscious awareness. As expressive arts therapist and scholar Daria Halprin (2003) so eloquently stated:

> Just as the physical body gives us a literal and concrete structure that expresses who we are, so every part and function of the body can also be understood as metaphors for the expression of our being. We feel and observe our life experiences through our bodies…Our bodies contain our life stories just as they contain bones, muscle, organs, nerves, and blood. (p. 17)

Thus, through arts, movement, meditation, and other embodied practices, we can reconnect with the deeply embedded wisdom, metaphors, and stories we carry within our bodies, and consciously invite them into the healing process.

The practice of sitting meditation is, in itself, an inherently embodied practice, though it is most often described as a technique for working with the mind. However, psychologists working with mindfulness and meditation practices in a Western context are beginning to recognize the fundamental mind-body connection, as Olendzki (2010) described:

> It is not just that the mind depends upon the body, but the body also depends upon the mind, and both co-arise, co-create, and co-define one another. Furthermore, at the level of carefully examined lived experience, it might not be very useful to make a distinction between the two. (p. 12)

Traditional Buddhist meditation teachings and practices emphasized the interconnection of body, speech, and mind in mindfulness and awareness practices, with mindfulness of body as the first and most basic foundation of mindfulness (Analayo, 2003; Koller & Koller, 1991). While these traditional teachings certainly ground meditation practice in the physical body, several contemporary scholars and meditation teachers have also noted and emphasized the embodied nature of meditation practice. For example, psychologist John Welwood (2000) brought special attention to what he termed the "body-mind" in his synthesis of Buddhist and Western psychologies. Specifically, he explained that:

> Underneath the conceptual mind is a wider kind of body-mind sensing/knowing that operates in a subtler, background way…We can recognize this level of body-mind through a diffuse type of attention that can tune into subtle feeling and intuition, energy flow, and a sense of interrelatedness with all of creation. (Welwood, 2000, p. 6)

Perhaps most interesting for the themes of this book are the enormous creative possibilities that begin to arise as we attend to our own embodiment, as Welwood (2000) observed:

> The body-mind, as a dynamic field of energy, is inherently attuned to the larger patterns and flows of the universe. Out of this attunement emerge sudden and surprising insights, creative inspirations and discoveries, and larger, transpersonal qualities, such as clarity, compassion, joy, or spontaneity. (pp. 6–7)

This understanding of the potentiality that dwells within our embodiment parallels the traits of openness to experience, expressiveness, and a deep engagement with the world that humanistic psychologists Rogers (1961), Maslow (1962/2011), and May (1975) identified with creative people and the drive toward creativity.

Summary

This chapter began with a personal introduction to how the practice of mindfulness and contemplative arts has influenced me, both on a personal level and as a teacher and scholar. It then provided definitions for the key terms and concepts that will be discussed throughout the book, including mindfulness, creativity, and contemplative arts. With these definitions in mind, the following sections discussed the interconnections between these concepts, including specifically how mindfulness and contemplative arts practice relate to creativity. It also emphasized the importance of embodiment and embodied awareness for both mindfulness and creativity. This chapter sets the stage for the following chapter, which takes a deeper dive into the theoretical underpinnings and research literature on mindfulness and creativity in organizational contexts.

References

Agnoli, S., Vanucci, M., Pelagatti, C., & Corazza, G. E. (2018). Exploring the link between mind wandering, mindfulness, and creativity: A multidimensional approach. *Creativity Research Journal, 30*(1), 41–53. https://doi.org/10.1080/10400419.2018.1411423

Amabile, T. M. (1996). *Creativity in context.* Boulder, CO: Westview Press.

Analayo, B. (2003). *Satipatthana: The direct path to realization.* Cambridge, UK: Windhorse Publications.

Baas, M., Nevicka, B., & Ten Velden, F. S. (2014). Specific mindfulness skills differentially predict creative performance. *Personality and Social Psychology Bulletin, 40*(9), 1092–1106.

Barner, C. P., & Barner, R. W. (2012). Mindfulness, openness to experience, and transformational learning. In *The Oxford handbook of reciprocal adult development and learning* (2nd ed.). https://doi.org/10.1093/oxfordhb/9780199736300.013.0087

Barratt, B. B. (2010). *The emergence of somatic psychology and bodymind therapy.* New York, NY: Palgrave Macmillan.

Berkovich-Ohana, A., Glicksohn, J., Ben-Soussan, T. D., & Goldstein, A. (2017). Creativity is enhanced by long-term mindfulness training and is negatively correlated with trait default-mode-related low-gamma inter-hemispheric connectivity. *Mindfulness, 8*(3), 717–727. https://doi.org/10.1007/s12671-016-0649-y.

Chesshire, C. (2009). *The illustrated encyclopedia of Japanese gardening.* London, UK: Hermes House.

Colzato, L. S., Ozturk, A., & Hommel, B. (2012). Meditate to create: The impact of focused-attention and open-monitoring training on convergent and divergent thinking. *Frontiers in Psychology, 3*, 116. https://doi.org/10.3389/fpsyg.2012.00116

Crescentini, C., & Capurso, V. (2015). Mindfulness meditation and explicit and implicit indicators of personality and self-concept changes. *Frontiers in Psychology, 6*(44). https://doi.org/10.3389/fpsyg.2015.00044

Csikszentmihalyi, M. (1990). *Flow: The psychology of optimal experience.* New York, NY: HarperCollins.

Csikszentmihalyi, M. (1996/2013). *Creativity: The psychology of discovery and invention.* New York, NY: HarperCollins.

Csikszentmihalyi, M. (1999). Implications of a systems perspective for the study of creativity. In R. J. Sternberg (Ed.), *Handbook of creativity* (pp. 313–335). New York, NY: Cambridge University Press.

Daido Loori, J. (2004). *The Zen of creativity: Cultivating your artistic life.* New York, NY: Ballantine Books.

Damasio, A. (1999). *The feeling of what happens: Body and emotion in the making of consciousness.* New York, NY: Houghton Mifflin Harcourt.

Damasio, A. (2010). *Self comes to mind: Constructing the conscious brain.* New York, NY: Vintage Books.

Davis, D. M., & Hayes, J. A. (2011). What are the benefits of mindfulness? A practice review of psychotherapy-related research. *Psychotherapy, 48*(2), 198–208. https://doi.org/10.1037/a0022062

Dreyfus, H. L. (1996). The current relevance of Merleau-Ponty's phenomenology of embodiment. The Electronic Journal of Analytic Philosophy, 4. Retrieved from http://ejap.louisiana.edu/ejap/1996.spring/dreyfus.1996.spring.html.

Fogel, A. (2009). *Body sense: The science and practice of embodied self-awareness.* New York, NY: Norton.

Gelb, D. (Director). (2017, February 17). Jeong Kwan [Television series episode]. In A. Fried & D. Gelb (Executive producers), *Chef's table* (Season 3, Episode 1). Los Gatos, CA: Netflix.

Gendlin, E. T. (1978). *Focusing.* New York, NY: Random House.

Gillam, T. (2018). *Creativity, wellbeing and mental health practice.* London, UK: Palgrave Macmillan.

Goldberg, N. (1986). *Writing down the bones.* Boston, MA: Shambhala Publications.

Guilford, J. P. (1967). Creativity: Yesterday, today and tomorrow. *The Journal of Creative Behavior, 1*(1), 3–14. https://doi.org/10.1002/j.2162-6057.1967.tb00002.x

Haidt, J. (2006). *The happiness hypothesis: Finding modern truth in ancient wisdom.* New York, NY: Basic Books.

Halprin, D. (2003). *The expressive body in life, art and therapy: Working with movement, metaphor and meaning.* Philadelphia, PA: Jessica Kingsley Publishers.

Hyland, P. K., Lee, R. A., & Mills, M. J. (2015). Mindfulness at work: A new approach to improving individual and organizational performance. *Industrial and Organizational Psychology, 8*(4), 576–602. https://doi.org/10.1017/iop.2015.41

James, K., & Drown, D. (2012). Organizations and creativity: Trends in research, status of education and practice, agenda for the future. In M. Mumford (Ed.), *Handbook of organizational creativity* (pp. 17–38). San Diego, CA: Academic Press.

Janson, H. W. (1986). *History of art* (3rd ed.). New York, NY: Harry N. Abrams.

Kabat-Zinn, J. (1991). *Full catastrophe living: Using the wisdom of your body and mind to face stress, pain, and illness.* New York, NY: Delta Trade Paperbacks.

Kabat-Zinn, J. (1994). *Wherever you go, there you are: Mindfulness meditation in everyday life.* New York, NY: Hyperion Books.

Karr, A., & Wood, M. (2011). *The practice of contemplative photography: Seeing the world with fresh eyes.* Boston, MA: Shambhala Publications.

Kaufman, J. C., & Beghetto, R. A. (2009). Beyond big and little: The four C model of creativity. *Review of General Psychology, 13*(1), 1–12. https://doi.org/10.1037/a0013688

Kaufman, S. B. (2013). Opening up openness to experience: A four-factor model and relations to creative achievement in the arts and sciences. *The Journal of Creative Behavior, 47*(4), 233–255. https://doi.org/10.1002/jocb.33

Kaufman, S. B., & Gregoire, C. (2015). *Wired to create: Unraveling the mysteries of the creative mind*. New York, NY: Perigee.

Kaufman, S. B., Quilty, L. C., Grazioplene, R. G., Hirsh, J. B., Gray, J. R., Peterson, J. B., & DeYoung, C. G. (2016). Openness to experience and intellect differentially predict creative achievement in the arts and sciences. *Journal of Personality, 84*(2), 248–258. https://doi.org/10.1111/jopy.12156

Kaviani, H., & Hatami, N. (2016). Link between mindfulness and personality-related factors including empathy, theory of mind, openness, pro-social behaviour and suggestibility. *Clinical Depression, 2*, 119. https://doi.org/10.4172/2572-0791.1000119

Koller, J. M., & Koller, P. (1991). *A sourcebook in Asian philosophy*. Upper Saddle River, NJ: Prentice Hall.

Koren, L. (1994). *Wabi sabi for artists, designers, poets and philosophers*. Berkeley, CA: Stone Bridge Press.

Kornfield, J. (2008). *The wise heart: A guide to the universal teachings of Buddhist psychology*. New York, NY: Bantam Books.

Kozbelt, A., Beghetto, R. A., & Runco, M. A. (2010). Theories of creativity. In J. C. Kaufman & R. J. Sternberg (Eds.), *The Cambridge handbook of creativity* (pp. 20–47). New York, NY: Cambridge University Press.

Kudesia, R. S. (2015). Mindfulness and creativity in the workplace. In J. Reb & P. Atkins (Eds.), *Mindfulness in organizations: Foundations, research, and applications* (Cambridge Companions to Management) (pp. 190–212). Cambridge: Cambridge University Press. https://doi.org/10.1017/CBO9781107587793.010

Langer, E. (1989/2014). *Mindfulness* (25th anniversary ed.). Boston, MA: Da Capo Press.

Langer, E. (2005). *On becoming an artist—Reinventing yourself through mindful creativity*. New York, NY: Ballantine Books.

Langer, E. (2014, March). Mindfulness in the age of complexity. *Harvard Business Review*, pp. 68–73. Retrieved from https://hbr.org/2014/03/mindfulness-in-the-age-of-complexity

Lebuda, I., Zabelina, D. L., & Karwowski, M. (2016). Mind full of ideas: A meta-analysis of the mindfulness–creativity link. *Personality and Individual Differences, 93*, 22–26. https://doi.org/10.1016/j.paid.2015.09.040.

Marion, R. (2012). Leadership of creativity: Entity-based, relational, and complexity perspectives. In M. Mumford (Ed.), *Handbook of organizational creativity* (pp. 457–479). San Diego, CA: Academic Press.

Maslow, A. (1962/2011). *Toward a psychology of being*. Mansfield Centre, CT: Martino Publishing.

May, R. (1975). *The courage to create*. New York, NY: W. W. Norton & Co.

McQuade, J., & Hall, M. (2015). *Looking and seeing: Nalanda Miksang contemplative photography*. Madison, WI: Drala Publishing.

Merleau-Ponty, M. (1948/2004). *The world of perception* (O. Davis, Trans.). New York, NY: Routledge.

Merleau-Ponty, M. (1964). Eye and mind. In J. E. Edie (Ed.), *The primacy of perception* (C. Dallery, Trans., pp. 159–190). Evanston, IL: Northwestern University Press.

Müller, B. C. N., Gerasimova, A., & Ritter, S. M. (2016). Concentrative meditation influences creativity by increasing cognitive flexibility. *Psychology of Aesthetics, Creativity, and the Arts, 10*(3), 278–286. https://doi.org/10.1037/a0040335

Mumford, M. D., Hester, K. S., & Robledo, I. C. (2012). Creativity in organizations: Importance and approaches. In M. Mumford (Ed.), *Handbook of organizational creativity* (pp. 3–16). San Diego, CA: Academic Press.

Okuda, S., Runco, M., & Berger, D. (1991). Creativity and the finding and solving of real-world problems. *Journal of Psychoeducational Assessment, 9*(1), 45–53.

Olendzki, A. (2010). *Unlimiting mind: The radically experiential psychology of Buddhism*. Boston, MA: Wisdom Publications.

Plucker, J. A., & Makel, M. C. (2010). Assessment of creativity. In J. C. Kaufman & R. J. Sternberg (Eds.), *The Cambridge handbook of creativity* (pp. 48–73). New York, NY: Cambridge University Press.

Pritzker, S. (2011). Zen. In M. A. Runco & S. R. Pritzker (Eds.), *Encyclopedia of creativity* (Vol. 2, 2nd ed., pp. 539–543). San Diego, CA: Academic Press.

Raskin, J. D. (2012). Evolutionary constructivism and humanistic psychology. *Journal of Theoretical and Philosophical Psychology, 32*, 119–133.

Richards, R. (Ed.). (2007). *Everyday creativity and new views of human nature: Psychological, social, and spiritual perspectives*. Washington, DC: American Psychological Association.

Richards, R. (2010). Everyday creativity: Process and way of life—Four key issues. In J. C. Kaufman & R. J. Sternberg (Eds.), *The Cambridge handbook of creativity* (pp. 189–215). New York, NY: Cambridge University Press.

Richards, R. (2018). *Everyday creativity and the healthy mind: Dynamic new paths for self and society*. London, UK: Palgrave Macmillan.

Rogers, C. (1961). *On becoming a person: A therapist's view of psychotherapy*. New York, NY: Houghton Mifflin Company.

Romanyshyn, R. D. (2012). The necessity for the humanities in psychology: The psychologist and his/her shadow. *The Humanistic Psychologist, 40*, 234–245. https://doi.org/10.1080/08873267.2012.696504

Rothouse, M. (2018). *Facilitating team creativity and collaboration using mindfulness and contemplative arts* (Doctoral dissertation). Retrieved from ProQuest Dissertations and Theses (Order No. 10823776).

Runco, M. A. (Ed.). (1994). *Problem finding, problem solving, and creativity.* Norwood, NJ: Ablex.

Saitzyk, S. (2013). *Place your thoughts here: Meditation for the creative mind.* Los Angeles, CA: First Thought Press.

Sartwell, C. (2012). Beauty. In *Stanford Encyclopedia of Philosophy.* Retrieved from http://plato.stanford.edu/entries/beauty/

Scharmer, C. O. (2009). *Theory U: Leading from the future as it emerges.* San Francisco, CA: Berrett-Koehler Publishers, Inc.

Scharmer, C. O. (2013, July 9). Uncovering the blind spot of leadership. Retrieved from http://www.dailygood.org/story/450/uncovering-the-blind-spot-of-leadership-c-otto-scharmer/

Schwarz, R. (2015, December). What the research tells us about team creativity and innovation. *Harvard Business Review.* Retrieved from https://hbr.org/2015/12/what-the-research-tells-us-about-team-creativity-and-innovation

Shi, B., Dai, D. Y., & Lu, Y. (2016, May). Openness to experience as a moderator of the relationship between intelligence and creative thinking: A study of Chinese children in urban and rural areas. *Frontiers in Psychology, 7*, 641. https://doi.org/10.3389/fpsyg.2016.00641

Siegel, D. (2007). *The mindful brain: Reflection and attunement in the cultivation of well-being.* New York, NY: W. W. Norton & Co.

Siegel, D. (2010). *The mindful therapist: A clinician's guide to mindsight and neural integration.* New York, NY: W. W. Norton & Co.

Silvia, P. J., Nusbaum, E. C., Berg, C., Martin, C., & O'Connor, A. (2009). Openness to experience, plasticity, and creativity: Exploring lower-order, higher-order, and interactive effects. *Journal of Research in Personality, 43*(6), 1087–1090. https://doi.org/10.1016/j.jrp.2009.04.015

Simonton, D. K. (2012). Fields, domains, and individuals. In M. Mumford (Ed.), *Handbook of organizational creativity* (pp. 67–86). San Diego, CA: Academic Press.

Slater, B. H. (n.d.). Aesthetics. In *Internet Encyclopedia of Philosophy.* Retrieved from http://www.iep.utm.edu/aestheti/

Suzuki, S. (1970/2007). *Zen mind, beginner's mind.* Boston, MA: Weatherhill.

Thera, N. (1994). *The foundations of mindfulness: Satipatthana sutta.* Retrieved from http://www.accesstoinsight.org/lib/authors/nyanasatta/wheel019.html

Trungpa, C. (1996/2008). *True perception: The path of dharma art*. Boston, MA: Shambhala Publications.

Varela, F. J., Thompson, E., & Rosch, E. (1991). *The embodied mind: Cognitive science and human experience*. Boston, MA: MIT Press.

Welwood, J. (2000). *Toward a psychology of awakening: Buddhism, psychotherapy, and the path of personal and spiritual transformation*. Boston, MA: Shambhala Publications.

Zehr, H. (2005). *The little book of contemplative photography: Seeing with wonder, respect, and humility*. Intercourse, PA: Good Books.

CHAPTER 3

Contemporary Research on Creativity, Collaboration, and Mindfulness in Teams and Organizations

Abstract This chapter surveys contemporary research on creativity, collaboration, and mindfulness among teams and organizations, including the factors that both support and hinder team creativity and collaboration. It also describes how mindfulness protocols and arts-based programs are currently being implemented in a number of companies and organizations to support well being, creativity, and collaboration. The research presented here provides a theoretical and scholarly groundwork for the material and exercises discussed in the following chapters.

Keywords Creativity research • Collaboration • Mindfulness • Organizational creativity • Arts-based programs

The Mindful Business Meeting

For a number of years, I served on the governing council of a meditation center in Austin, Texas. In keeping with the center's teachings on mindfulness in daily life and governance, we began our monthly meetings with a few minutes of silent meditation practice, sitting in a circle, followed by a personal check-in of how each member was doing and what was happening in their lives, before turning to the business of the meeting. By

M. J. Rothouse, *A Mindful Approach to Team Creativity and Collaboration in Organizations*, Palgrave Studies in Creativity and Innovation in Organizations,
https://doi.org/10.1007/978-3-030-47675-5_3

beginning our meetings in this way, each person had the opportunity to arrive, physically and mentally, and to become grounded in the present-moment experience of the meeting. Any personal issues, challenges, or positive news could be shared with the group before diving into the specifics of the meeting agenda.

In my experience, this practice allowed for a more focused and productive meeting, more genuine communication, and a sense of care and concern to develop between the members, both in the present moment and over time. As we discussed particular agenda items during the meetings, each person had the opportunity to speak about whatever issue was being discussed, to voice their perspectives and concerns, and be fully heard. Once all voices had been heard, the group voted either to take a particular action or to continue researching the issue and gathering information for a later vote.

This mindfulness-based process allowed for a strong degree of trust and collaboration within the group that also allowed for differing perspectives and dissenting opinions, and often generated very thoughtful and creative solutions rather than hasty decisions. I have used this model of beginning with a few minutes of silent or guided meditation in other types of organizational meetings in other contexts that I have facilitated or been a part of, and I find that it sets a very different tone from meetings that get "straight to business." It offers the potential for a greater sense of ease, relaxation, and openness among whatever group is assembled for whatever purpose, particularly when there are difficult or challenging items on the agenda for discussion.

Research on Team Creativity and Collaboration

This chapter surveys contemporary research on creativity, collaboration, and mindfulness among teams and organizations, including the factors that both support and hinder team creativity and collaboration, as well as how mindfulness protocols are currently being implemented in a number of companies and organizations. It also surveys existing research on how arts-based programs are being used to support creativity in organizations. The research presented in this chapter provides a theoretical and scholarly groundwork for the material and exercises discussed in the following chapters.

Since the turn of the century, researchers studying organizational leadership and creativity have identified a number of conditions and dynamics that influence workplace creativity and collaboration (Alencar, 2012; Anderson & Adams, 2016, 2019; Burkus, 2013; George, 2007; James & Drown, 2012; Müller & Ulrich, 2013; Mumford & Todd, 2020; Reiter-Palmon, 2018; Reiter-Palmon, Wigert & de Vreede, 2012; Sawyer, 2017; Zhou & Hoever, 2014). Organizational creativity and collaboration is a complex phenomenon, which is influenced by many different factors, both on the level of the individual and that of the wider group, team, and organization (Zhou & Hoever, 2014).

Within individuals, mood and emotion play an important role in workplace creativity (De Dreu, Baas, & Nijstad, 2012; To & Fisher, 2019), along with possession of the necessary skills, expertise, engagement, a sense of creative autonomy, and a blend of intrinsic and extrinsic motivation (Amabile, 1996, 1998; Conti & Amabile, 2011; Csikszentmihalyi, 1990, 1996/2013; Mumford, Todd, Higgs, & Martin, 2020; Wang, 2016). Specifically, individual creativity in the workplace is generally enhanced by positive emotion and affect as well as activating moods (De Dreu et al., 2012), though this relationship is complex and negative moods are also recognized to be both inevitable and necessary in the creative process (To & Fisher, 2019). Individual creativity also benefits from goals that foster both challenge and a high level of task engagement, along with a blend of intrinsic and extrinsic motivation (Amabile, 1996, 1998; Conti & Amabile, 2011). On the other hand, work environments characterized by a lack of autonomy, psychological safety, and trust are negatively associated with individual creativity in organizational settings, as described by Alencar (2012) and reaffirmed by the recent O.C. Tanner 2020 Global Culture Survey ("Teams," 2019).

Group-level dynamics affecting team creativity and collaboration include a number of different factors. These include the overall culture and climate of the organization and its leadership (Anderson & Adams, 2016, 2019; Auernhammer & Hall, 2014; Holden & Hewison, 2011; Joo, McLean, & Yang, 2013; Pater, 2013; Zhou & George, 2003), which will be discussed in more depth in Chap. 8. Another important element is the degree of diversity within the group in terms of perspectives, experience, and background (Amabile & Khaire, 2008; Milliken, Bartel, & Kurtzberg, 2003; Nemeth & Nemeth-Brown, 2003; Oades-Sese & Esquivel, 2011; Schwarz, 2015; Stasser & Birchmeier, 2003). Other important individual and contextual factors include workspace design (Blakey, 2015; Moultrie et al., 2007; Suckley & Nicholson, 2018), goal setting and feedback on performance (Zhou & Shalley, 2003), and psychological safety, empathy, and trust (Alencar, 2012; Duhigg, 2016; Edmondson, 2004, 2019; John-Steiner, 2000, 2011; Miyashiro, 2011; Rozovsky, 2015).

With respect to team creativity and collaboration specifically, Reiter-Palmon et al. (2012) identified several major factors affecting team dynamics, including team composition and diversity; social processes such as communication, psychological safety, trust, and cohesion; and cognitive processes including the ways teams approach idea generation, brainstorming, creative problem solving, problem construction, and team reflexivity. Indeed, they strongly emphasized the fundamental importance of collaboration for creative teamwork:

> Studies evaluating creativity and innovation in organizational settings find that collaboration is critical for team creativity and innovation…These results support the notion that collaboration facilitates open communication and interactions, which contribute to team creativity and innovation. Further, inclusive and comprehensive decision making allows team members to take advantage of the multiple perspectives from team members with varying expertise, perspectives, and experiences. (Reiter-Palmon et al., 2012, p. 303)

As this section of the chapter illustrates, the factors influencing team creativity and collaboration are complex and multifaceted, but most scholars agree that collaboration is essential for group creativity and organizational innovation.

Mindfulness in the Workplace

With a growing interest in mindfulness and meditation over the last few decades, the amount of research and news coverage of mindfulness has grown exponentially. From the early 1970s to 2015, the number of academic research publications focusing on meditation and mindfulness has grown from nearly none to over 1000 per year, while the number of news articles has risen to more than 30,000 per year (Van Dam et al., 2018). Many studies have chronicled the potential benefits of meditation and mindfulness practice for mental and physical health, ranging from relaxation and stress resilience to improved immune functioning and neuroplasticity (Siegel, 2011). As the so-called mindfulness revolution (Boyce, 2011; Pickert, 2014) has begun to permeate the Western psyche, business leaders have also started to explore how mindfulness may affect productivity, employee engagement, organizational leadership, and well-being in the workplace, as well as creativity and innovation.

Mindfulness researchers have explored an array of potential benefits of mindfulness relevant to workplace functioning and organizational behavior in areas ranging from relational skills like communication, empathy, and leadership to improved executive functioning, attention, task performance, decision-making, employee engagement, and teamwork (Good, et al., 2016; Hyland, Lee, & Mills, 2015).

Mindfulness and Creativity in Organizations

In recent years, creativity and organizational psychology researchers have begun to explore the relationships between mindfulness and creativity, including in organizational contexts. As noted in the previous chapter, Harvard psychologist Ellen Langer (1989/2014, 2005, 2014) has devoted the majority of her career and research to the study of mindfulness, including the relationships between mindfulness and creativity, mindfulness in the workplace, and mindful leadership. Her research focusing on mindfulness and creativity in organizations emphasizes the importance of attention and how mindfulness supports active noticing and engagement, which in turn improves performance. Her research suggests that mindfulness training supports focused attention and engagement in the task at hand, thus pulling people out of their often distracted or mindless work routines (Langer, 2014).

Langer's research on mindfulness in organizational contexts also emphasizes how mindfulness training allows people to move beyond binary, right versus wrong thinking to a broader range of possibilities, as well as to shift more easily between contexts, which can lead to greater creativity and innovation rather than a rote reliance on existing processes and procedures. Describing the relevance of mindfulness for workplace creativity and engagement, Langer (1989/2014) observed:

> The ability to shift contexts may be just as valuable to a manager or on the assembly line as it is to an artist or physicist. Fatigue, conflict, and burnout can all result from being mired in old categories, trapped by old mind-sets....For employer and employee alike, mindfulness may increase flexibility, productivity, innovation, leadership ability, and satisfaction. (p. 131)

Along with a group of colleagues, she developed the Langer Mindfulness Scale, a 14-item mindfulness assessment specifically focusing on creativity in group and organizational settings, including "novelty seeking, novelty producing, engagement, and flexibility" (Pirson, Langer, Bodner & Zilcha-Mano, 2012, p. 6). A good portion of Langer's (1989/2014, 2005, 2014) work has emphasized the applications of mindfulness to professional and organizational creativity, emphasizing the effects of mindfulness training on attention, awareness, and cognitive flexibility.

Recent doctoral research into mindfulness and creativity has deepened the conversation about which aspects of mindfulness support creative functioning in the workplace, and how this actually works. One such study examined the relationships between mindfulness, stress, and creativity by analyzing the results of 25 prior studies, finding that workplace mindfulness programs not only helped to reduce stress but also supported motivation and employee engagement, while also increasing cognitive flexibility and creativity (Sand, 2015). The researcher noted that "mindfulness presents a competency that can be developed, fostered, and managed like any other. Mindful employees have the competencies of being aware, attentive, accepting and non-judgmental in ways that enable the exploration of new mindsets, information and perspectives" (Sand, 2015, p. 142).

Two other studies conducted within real-world organizational settings examined the effects of meditation and mindfulness practice on several measures of individual- and group-level creativity in the workplace. Holm (2014) demonstrated statistically significant effects of a focused-technique meditation practice on mindfulness, creativity, and well-being among employees in three different organizations, with positive increases in teamwork and connection as well as productivity and innovation. Similarly, Byrne (2017) found increases in both individual creative workplace functioning and measures of team creativity and collaboration following a five-week mindfulness training. Based on the results of her study, Byrne (2017) also developed a theoretical model describing the effects of mindfulness practice on workgroup creativity showing how mindfulness training supports increased attention and awareness, which in turn allows for greater cognitive flexibility and access to the unconscious, leading to more receptivity to novel ideas from self and group members, which directly affects creative output. The results of Byrne's study (which I learned of only after I had completed my own and was finalizing my dissertation) bear strong parallels to my own research findings, affirming a strong connection between mindfulness practice and workplace creativity.

My doctoral research (Rothouse, 2018), also conducted within a functioning organization, lent further support to the emerging research, described above, into the relationships between mindfulness and workplace creativity. Through a combination of interviews, focus groups, and surveys to assess the perceived effects of a mindfulness and contemplative arts workshop process on team creativity and collaboration, my research suggested that such a process could be particularly beneficial for cultivating individual-level mindfulness, developing greater trust and open communication within teams, and shifting the energy when the creative process has stalled. Specifically, with respect to individual-level mindfulness, one of the co-researchers in my study observed, "I will be more mindful of my own creativity and approach to challenges and projects," while another commented on the process as a whole, "once trust grew and people could be honest, ideas and communication opened up" (Rothouse, 2018, p. 133). The model I developed based on my dissertation research (presented in Chap. 1 of this book) expands upon recent research exploring the relationship between creativity and mindfulness in teams and organizations (Baas, Nevicka, & Ten Velden, 2014; Byrne, 2017; Holm, 2014; Müller, Gerasimova, & Ritter, 2016; Sand, 2015).

Mindfulness Programs in Organizations

As researchers and organizational leaders have begun to realize the potential benefits of mindfulness in the workplace, a number of organizations have started to implement mindfulness programs for their employees and constituents. Indeed, according to Erlich (2015):

> Over a dozen Fortune 500 organizations are teaching mindfulness to employees and it is also being taught by the U.S. Army and in public schools and MBA programs. Companies are finding significant benefits, including improved focus, decision-making, creativity, and learning; increased communication, collaboration, and productivity; enriched emotional intelligence, well-being, and client relationships; higher job satisfaction and engagement. (p. 23)

Indeed, a number of major corporations including Google, Aetna, General Mills, and Patagonia have begun to incorporate mindfulness into their workplace cultures (Gelles, 2015).

One of the most well-known and well-established workplace mindfulness programs is the *Search Inside Yourself* curriculum created by Chade-Meng Tan (2012, 2015) at Google. *Search Inside Yourself* incorporated theories and practices from Goleman's (1995/2005, 2011) work on emotional intelligence as well as Kabat-Zinn's (1991, 1994) Mindfulness-Based Stress Reduction (MBSR) program, along with insights from neuroscience research to support self-awareness, attention management, and mindfulness in the workplace (Tan, 2012). With data from hundreds of Google employees who have now completed the program, the major reported benefits include improved interpersonal communication and stress management as well as creativity and leadership (Tan, 2015). While initially created for Google employees, the *Search Inside Yourself* program spawned the Search Inside Yourself Leadership Institute, which now offers the program as a professional development training to the wider public, including both individuals and organizations.

Mindfulness and Artistic Practices in Organizational Contexts

The Role of Artistic Practice and Expressive Arts in Group Creativity

The use of arts-based and expressive arts practices adds an important dimension to organizational creativity research and practice related to mindfulness and contemplative arts. As I described in my dissertation:

> Arts-based approaches can stimulate new ways of thinking and looking at business-related problems, leading to greater innovation. Art and artistic practices provide a doorway into ways of knowing that allow people working in organizational contexts to tap into aesthetic and intuitive knowledge as opposed to the more conventional linear and logical modes of thinking most often employed in organizational contexts. A number of researchers, business leaders, and consultants in recent years have applied arts-based approaches to organizational creativity and collaboration, with much success. (Rothouse, 2018, p. 42)

The field of expressive arts has demonstrated the therapeutic value of creativity for individuals and groups. Expressive arts is a branch of psychology that combines the therapeutic insights and techniques of art therapy with a variety of artistic forms to facilitate psychological healing, self-awareness, and transformation (Donohue, 2011; Levine & Levine, 1999, 2011; Rogers, 1993, 2011). As described by International Expressive Arts Therapy Association (IEATA), "The expressive arts combine the visual arts, movement, drama, music, writing and other creative processes to foster deep personal growth and community development" ("Who We Are," 2014).

In group settings, expressive arts activities have proven useful in the form of workshops, classrooms, and workplaces both for individual enrichment and creativity and to support group communication and cohesion (Avalon, 2006; Goslin-Jones, 2010, 2011; Goslin-Jones & Herron, 2016; Rogers, 1993, 2011). In addition, scholar-practitioners such as Levine and Levine (2011) have written extensively about the benefits of using expressive arts not only for group healing from collective trauma and injustice, but also for social change. Expressive arts and other artistic practices thus offer a unique pathway to access creative thinking, insight, and meaningful change in the world which are extremely relevant to organizations that wish to foster innovation through team creativity and collaboration.

Another important figure who has used a combination of mindfulness and artistic approaches to address organizational creativity is David Whyte (1994/2002, 2001, 2016), a poet who has made a career of using the language of poetry, myth, and literature to explore questions of meaning and identity for people working in organizations. He has worked with executives from a number of large companies including American Express, Xerox, and Boeing to facilitate new perspectives and ways of addressing complex organizational challenges.

Up to this point, a small number of innovators have applied mindfulness and contemplative arts practices in interesting ways to creative and organizational contexts. These include avant-garde composer Pauline Oliveros, who created a series of instructions for group musical improvisation called the *Sonic Meditations* (1974). Oliveros' groundbreaking work, based in the principles of non-judgmental awareness deep listening (as described in O'Brien, 2016 and Osborne, 2000) also spawned the Deep Listening Institute. Oliveros' work with the practice of sonic meditation will be discussed in more depth, and will be presented as a contemplative arts exercise, in Chap. 6.

Another group of pioneers in bringing contemplative arts practices to organizations are the creators of the Presencing Institute, including

Arawana Hayashi and Otto Scharmer, who combined techniques of Scharmer's Theory U model of organizational change with practices drawn from dance and theater to create a process called social presencing theater (Hayashi, 2017; Kleiner, 2017; Scharmer, 2009, 2013; "Social Presencing Theater," 2015). These practices emphasize mindfulness, awareness, and curiosity in service of organizational innovation, collaboration, and transformation.

Summary

Chapter 3 surveyed contemporary research on creativity, collaboration, and mindfulness in teams and organizations, beginning with an overview of the factors that either contribute to or inhibit team creativity and collaboration. It then reviewed research on mindfulness in the workplace and how mindfulness programs are currently being incorporated into organizational contexts and cultures. It also discussed how arts-based programs, including contemplative arts, are being used in organizations to support creativity and social change. With this contemporary research in mind, Chap. 4 will turn to the model I developed in my research, discussing the role of individual-level mindfulness in team creativity and collaboration, and presenting a series of exercises that can help to cultivate mindfulness in organizational settings.

References

Alencar, E. M. L. S. (2012). Creativity in organizations: Facilitators and inhibitors. In M. Mumford (Ed.), *Handbook of organizational creativity* (pp. 87–111). San Diego, CA: Academic Press.

Amabile, T. M. (1996). *Creativity in context*. Boulder, CO: Westview Press.

Amabile, T. M. (1998). A model for creativity and innovation in organizations. *Research in Organizational Behavior, 10*, 123–167.

Amabile, T. M., & Khaire, M. (2008, October). Creativity and the role of the leader. *Harvard Business Review*. Retrieved from https://hbr.org/2008/10/creativity-and-the-role-of-the-leader

Anderson, R. J., & Adams, W. A. (2016). *Mastering leadership: An integrated framework for breakthrough performance and extraordinary business results*. Hoboken, NJ: John Wiley & Sons, Inc.

Anderson, R. J., & Adams, W. A. (2019). *Scaling leadership: Building organizational capability and capacity to create outcomes that matter most*. Hoboken, NJ: John Wiley & Sons, Inc.

Auernhammer, J., & Hall, H. (2014). Organizational culture in knowledge creation, creativity and innovation: Towards the Freiraum model. *Journal of Information Science, 40*(2), 154–166.

Avalon, A. (2006). *Arts in new directions: The development and application of a construct that uses the arts to promote transformation and self-actualization in health care and education/therapy* (Doctoral dissertation). Retrieved from ProQuest Dissertations and Theses (UMI No: 3240360).

Baas, M., Nevicka, B., & Ten Velden, F. S. (2014). Specific mindfulness skills differentially predict creative performance. *Personality and Social Psychology Bulletin, 40*(9), 1092–1106.

Blakey, J. D. (2015). *The impact of workspace on innovation* (Doctoral dissertation). Retrieved from ProQuest Dissertations and Theses (UMI No: 3702901).

Boyce, B. (Ed.). (2011). *The mindfulness revolution: Leading psychologists, scientists, artists, and meditation teachers on the power of mindfulness in everyday life.* Boulder, CO: Shambhala Publications.

Burkus, D. (2013). *Myths of creativity: The truth about how innovative companies and people generate great ideas.* Somerset, NJ: John Wiley & Sons, Inc.

Byrne, E. K. (2017). *Mindful creativity: An exploration of a mindfulness intervention on workgroup creativity* (Doctoral dissertation). Retrieved from ProQuest Dissertations and Theses (UMI No: 10271540).

Conti, R., & Amabile, T. M. (2011). Motivation. In M. A. Runco & S. R. Pritzker (Eds.), *Encyclopedia of creativity* (Vol. 1, 2nd ed., pp. 147–152). San Diego, CA: Academic Press.

Csikszentmihalyi, M. (1990). *Flow: The psychology of optimal experience.* New York, NY: HarperCollins.

Csikszentmihalyi, M. (1996/2013). *Creativity: The psychology of discovery and invention.* New York, NY: HarperCollins.

De Dreu, C. K. W., Baas, M., & Nijstad, B. A. (2012). The emotive roots of creativity: Basic and applied issues on affect and motivation. In M. Mumford (Ed.), *Handbook of organizational creativity* (pp. 217–240). San Diego, CA: Academic Press.

Donohue, K. T. (2011). Expressive arts therapy. In M. Runco & S. Pritzker (Eds.), *Encyclopedia of creativity* (Vol. 1, 2nd ed., pp. 497–501). San Diego, CA: Academic Press.

Duhigg, C. (2016, February 25). What Google learned from its quest to build a perfect team. *The New York Times Magazine.* Retrieved from www.nytimes.com/2016/02/28/magazine/what-google-learned-from-its-quest-to-build-the-perfect-team.html

Edmondson, A. C. (2004). Psychological safety, trust, and learning in organizations: A group-level lens. In R. M. Kramer & K. S. Cook (Eds.), *Trust and distrust in organizations: Dilemmas and approaches* (pp. 239–272). New York, NY: Russell Sage Foundation.

Edmondson, A. C. (2019). *The fearless organization: Creating psychological safety in the workplace for learning, innovation, and growth.* Hoboken, NJ: John Wiley & Sons, Inc.

Erlich, J. (2015). Creating mindful leaders and organizations. *People + Strategy, 38*(3), 22–25.

Gelles, D. (2015). *Mindful work: How meditation is changing business from the inside out.* Boston: Houghton Mifflin Harcourt.

George, J. (2007). Creativity in organizations. *The Academy of Management Annals, 1*(1), 439–477. https://doi.org/10.1080/078559814

Goleman, D. (1995/2005). *Emotional intelligence: Why it can matter more than IQ* (10th anniversary ed.). New York, NY: Bantam Books.

Goleman, D. (2011). *Leadership: The power of emotional intelligence.* Florence, MA: More Than Sound.

Good, D. J., Lyddy, C. J., Glomb, T. M., Bono, J. E., Brown, K. W., Duffy, M. K., … Lazar, S. W. (2016). Contemplating mindfulness at work: An integrative review. *Journal of Management, 42*(1), 114–142. https://doi.org/10.1177/0149206315617003

Goslin-Jones, T. (2010). *The perceived effects of person-centered expressive arts on one's work experience* (Doctoral dissertation). Retrieved from ProQuest Dissertations and Theses (UMI No: 3418296).

Goslin-Jones, T. (2011). Using expressive arts to transform the workplace. In N. Rogers (Ed.), *The creative connection for groups: Person-centered expressive arts for healing and social change* (pp. 354–357). Palo Alto, CA: Science and Behavior Books.

Goslin-Jones, T., & Herron, S. (2016). Cutting edge person-centered expressive arts. In C. Lago & D. Charr (Eds.), *The person-centered counseling and psychotherapy handbook* (pp. 199–211). New York, NY: Open University Press, McGraw-Hill Education.

Hayashi, A. (2017). *Social presencing theater.* Retrieved from https://arawana-hayashi.com

Holden, J., & Hewison, R. (2011). *Cultural leadership handbook: How to run a creative organization.* Farnham, UK: Ashgate Publishing Group.

Holm, M. (2014). Cultivating alternate mindsets to restructure the global economy by reducing stress and enhancing innovation. *The Business and Management Review, 5*(1), 279–289.

Hyland, P. K., Lee, R. A., & Mills, M. J. (2015). Mindfulness at work: A new approach to improving individual and organizational performance. *Industrial and Organizational Psychology, 8*(4), 576–602. https://doi.org/10.1017/iop.2015.41

James, K., & Drown, D. (2012). Organizations and creativity: Trends in research, status of education and practice, agenda for the future. In M. Mumford (Ed.), *Handbook of organizational creativity* (pp. 17–38). San Diego, CA: Academic Press.

John-Steiner, V. (2000). *Creative collaboration*. New York, NY: Oxford University Press.

John-Steiner, V. (2011). Collaboration. In M. Runco & S. Pritzker (Eds.), *Encyclopedia of creativity* (2nd ed., pp. 222–225). San Diego, CA: Academic Press.

Joo, B., McLean, G. N., & Yang, B. (2013). Creativity and human resource development: An integrative literature review and a conceptual framework for future research. *Human Resource Development Review, 12*(4), 390–421.

Kabat-Zinn, J. (1991). *Full catastrophe living: Using the wisdom of your body and mind to face stress, pain, and illness*. New York, NY: Delta Trade Paperbacks.

Kabat-Zinn, J. (1994). *Wherever you go, there you are: Mindfulness meditation in everyday life*. New York, NY: Hyperion Books.

Kleiner, A. (2017, August 7). What the body tells us about leadership. *Strategy + Business*. Retrieved from https://www.strategy-business.com/article/What-the-Body-Tells-Us-about-Leadership?gko=f5217

Langer, E. (1989/2014). *Mindfulness* (25th anniversary ed.). Boston, MA: Da Capo Press.

Langer, E. (2005). *On becoming an artist—Reinventing yourself through mindful creativity*. New York, NY: Ballantine Books.

Langer, E. (2014, March). Mindfulness in the age of complexity. *Harvard Business Review*, pp. 68–73. Retrieved from https://hbr.org/2014/03/mindfulness-in-the-age-of-complexity

Levine, E. G., & Levine, S. K. (Eds.). (2011). *Art in action: Expressive arts therapy and social change*. Philadelphia, PA: Jessica Kingsley Publishers.

Levine, S. K., & Levine, E. (Eds.). (1999). *Foundations of expressive arts therapy: Theoretical and clinical perspectives*. London, UK: J. Kingsley Publishers.

Milliken, F. J., Bartel, C. A., & Kurtzberg, T. R. (2003). Diversity and creativity in work groups: A dynamic perspective on the affective and cognitive processes that link diversity and performance. In P. B. Paulus & B. A. Nijstad (Eds.), *Group creativity: Innovation through collaboration* (pp. 32–62). New York, NY: Oxford University Press.

Miyashiro, M. R. (2011). *The empathy factor: Your competitive advantage for personal, team, and business success*. Encinitas, CA: Puddle Jumper Press.

Moultrie, J., Nilsson, M., Dissel, M., Haner, U. E., Janssen, S., & Van der Lugt, R. (2007). Innovation spaces: Towards a framework for understanding the role of the physical environment in innovation. *Creativity and Innovation Management, 16*(1), 53–65.

Müller, B. C. N., Gerasimova, A., & Ritter, S. M. (2016). Concentrative meditation influences creativity by increasing cognitive flexibility. *Psychology of Aesthetics, Creativity, and the Arts, 10*(3), 278–286. https://doi.org/10.1037/a0040335

Müller, S. D., & Ulrich, F. (2013). Creativity and information systems in a hypercompetitive environment: A literature review. *Communications of the Association for Information Systems, 32*. https://doi.org/10.17705/1CAIS.03207

Mumford, M. D., & Todd, E. M. (Eds.). (2020). *Creativity and innovation in organizations*. New York, NY: Routledge.
Mumford, M. D., Todd, E. M., Higgs, C., & Martin, R. (2020). What is needed to think creatively at work? Knowledge and skills. In M. D. Mumford & E. M. Todd (Eds.), *Creativity and innovation in organizations*. New York, NY: Routledge. Retrieved from https://books.google.com/books?id=30i8DwAAQBAJ&lpg=PT6&pg=PT70#v=onepage&q&f=false
Nemeth, C. J., & Nemeth-Brown, B. (2003). Better than individuals? The potential benefits of dissent and diversity for group creativity. In P. B. Paulus & B. A. Nijstad (Eds.), *Group creativity: Innovation through collaboration* (pp. 63–84). New York, NY: Oxford University Press.
Oades-Sese, G. V., & Esquivel, G. B. (2011). Cultural diversity and creativity. In M. A. Runco & S. R. Pritzker (Eds.), *Encyclopedia of creativity* (Vol. 1, 2nd ed., pp. 335–341). San Diego, CA: Academic Press.
O'Brien, K. (2016, December 9). Listening as activism: The "Sonic meditations" of Pauline Oliveros. *The New Yorker*. Retrieved from https://www.newyorker.com/culture/culture-desk/listening-as-activism-the-sonic-meditations-of-pauline-oliveros
Osborne, W. (2000). *Sounding the abyss of otherness: Pauline Oliveros' deep listening and the sonic meditations* (originally published as Chap. 3 of *Women making art*). Retrieved from http://www.osborne-conant.org/oliveros.htm
Pater, P. (2013, September). The art of creative, high-performance leadership. *Professional Safety*, pp. 37–40.
Pickert, K. (2014, January 23). The mindful revolution. *Time Magazine*. Retrieved from http://time.com/1556/the-mindful-revolution/
Pirson, M., Langer, E. J., Bodner, T., & Zilcha-Mano, S. (2012, October 8). The development and validation of the Langer mindfulness scale—Enabling a socio-cognitive perspective of mindfulness in organizational contexts. New York, NY: Fordham University School of Business Research Paper. https://doi.org/10.2139/ssrn.2158921
Reiter-Palmon, R. (Ed.). (2018). *Team creativity and innovation*. New York, NY: Oxford University Press.
Reiter-Palmon, R., Wigert, B., & de Vreede, T. (2012). Team creativity and innovation: The effect of group composition, social processes, and cognition. In M. D. Mumford (Ed.), *Handbook of organizational creativity* (pp. 295–326). Cambridge, UK: Academic Press.
Rogers, N. (1993). *The creative connection: Expressive arts as healing*. Palo Alto, CA: Science & Behavior Books, Inc.
Rogers, N. (2011). *The creative connection for groups: Person-centered expressive arts for healing and social change*. Palo Alto, CA: Science & Behavior Books, Inc.
Rothouse, M. (2018). *Facilitating team creativity and collaboration using mindfulness and contemplative arts* (Doctoral dissertation). Retrieved from ProQuest Dissertations and Theses (Order No. 10823776).

Rozovsky, J. (2015, November 17). The five keys to a successful Google team. Retrieved from https://rework.withgoogle.com/blog/five-keys-to-a-successful-google-team/

Sand, K. S. (2015). *Fostering creativity: Adopting mindfulness as an innovative approach* (Doctoral Dissertation). Retrieved from ProQuest Dissertations and Theses (Accession Order No. 3717293).

Sawyer, K. (2017). *Group genius: The creative power of collaboration* (2nd ed.). New York, NY: Basic Books.

Scharmer, C. O. (2009). *Theory U: Leading from the future as it emerges*. San Francisco, CA: Berrett-Koehler Publishers, Inc.

Scharmer, C. O. (2013, July 9). Uncovering the blind spot of leadership. Retrieved from http://www.dailygood.org/story/450/uncovering-the-blind-spot-of-leadership-c-otto-scharmer/

Schwarz, R. (2015, December). What the research tells us about team creativity and innovation. *Harvard Business Review*. Retrieved from https://hbr.org/2015/12/what-the-research-tells-us-about-team-creativity-and-innovation

Siegel, D. (2011). The proven benefits of mindfulness. In B. Boyce (Ed.), *The mindfulness revolution: Leading psychologists, scientists, artists, and meditation teachers on the power of mindfulness in daily life* (pp. 136–139). Boulder, CO: Shambhala Publications.

Social Presencing Theater: An embodied practice. (2015). Retrieved from https://www.presencing.com/social-presencing-theater

Stasser, G., & Birchmeier, Z. (2003). Group creativity and collective choice. In P. B. Paulus & B. A. Nijstad (Eds.), *Group creativity: Innovation through collaboration* (pp. 85–109). New York, NY: Oxford University Press.

Suckley, L., & Nicholson, J. (2018). Enhancing creativity through workspace design. In L. Martin & N. Wilson (Eds.), *The Palgrave handbook of creativity at work* (pp. 245–263). London, UK: Palgrave Macmillan. https://doi.org/10.1007/978-3-319-77350-6_12

Tan, C. (2012). *Search inside yourself: The unexpected path to achieving success, happiness (and world peace)*. New York, NY: HarperCollins.

Tan, C. (2015, December). Just 6 seconds of mindfulness can make you more effective. *Harvard Business Review*. Retrieved from https://hbr.org/2015/12/just-6-seconds-of-mindfulness-can-make-you-more-effective

"Teams." (2019). Retrieved December 26, 2019, from O.C. Tanner Global Culture Report website: https://www.octanner.com/global-culture-report/2020/leadership.html

To, M. L., & Fisher, C. D. (2019). Affective influences on creativity in teams: A multilevel regulatory perspective. In P. B. Paulus & B. A. Nijstad (Eds.), *The Oxford handbook of group creativity and innovation* (pp. 103–117). New York, NY: Oxford University Press.

Van Dam, N. T., van Vugt, M. K., Vago, D. R., Schmalzl, L., Saron, C. D., Olendzki, A., … Meyer, D. E. (2018). Mind the hype: A critical evaluation and prescriptive agenda for research on mindfulness and meditation. *Perspectives on Psychological Science, 13*(1), 36–61. https://doi.org/10.1177/1745691617709589

Wang, K. (2016). The effect of autonomy on team creativity and the moderating variables. *Journal of Creativity and Business Innovation, 2*, 160–171.

Who we are. (2014). Retrieved from http://ieata.org/who-we-are.html

Whyte, D. (1994/2002). *The heart aroused: Poetry and the preservation of the soul in corporate America*. New York, NY: Crown Business.

Whyte, D. (2001). *Crossing the unknown sea: Work as a pilgrimage of identity*. New York, NY: Riverhead Books.

Whyte, D. (2016, April 6). David Whyte—The conversational nature of reality (K. Tippett, Interviewer). [Audio file]. Retrieved from http://www.onbeing.org/program/david-whyte-the-conversational-nature-of-reality/8560

Zhou, J., & George, J. M. (2003). Awakening employee creativity: The role of leader in emotional intelligence. *The Leadership Quarterly, 14*(4–5), 545–586.

Zhou, J., & Hoever, I. J. (2014). Research on workplace creativity: A review and redirection. *Annual Review of Organizational Psychology and Organizational Behavior, 1*, 333–359. https://doi.org/10.1146/annurev-orgpsych-031413-091226

Zhou, J., & Shalley, C. E. (2003). Research on employee creativity: A critical review and directions for future research. *Research in Personnel and Human Resources Management, 22*, 165–217. Retrieved from https://psycnet.apa.org/record/2004-12778-004.

CHAPTER 4

Individual-Level Mindfulness and Organizational Creativity

Abstract This chapter surveys contemporary research on individual-level mindfulness in the workplace, illustrating how mindfulness and contemplative arts practices can support individual-level openness, receptivity, relaxation, well-being, self-awareness, and creativity in organizational contexts. The second part of the chapter introduces specific mindfulness and contemplative arts exercises designed to enhance mindfulness in the workplace on an individual level. The practices introduced in this chapter lay the foundation for the group- and team-level exercises presented in the following chapters. They can be used very effectively as standalone exercises, or to introduce and contextualize the exercises that appear later in the book.

Keywords Individual-level mindfulness • Organizational creativity • Openness • Receptivity • Self-awareness

A Little Mindfulness Goes a Long Way

A couple of years ago I facilitated a visioning and strategic planning initiative for the board of a non-profit foundation with the mission of maintaining and improving a community hike and bike trail. During the morning session, I led the group through a series of team-building exercises and

M. J. Rothouse, *A Mindful Approach to Team Creativity and Collaboration in Organizations*, Palgrave Studies in Creativity and Innovation in Organizations,
https://doi.org/10.1007/978-3-030-47675-5_4

conversations about the organization's vision, values, and future initiatives. After lunch, before turning to a discussion of the organization's mission statement and possible refinements to it, I invited the group to take a silent mindfulness walk outside along the trail for 10–15 minutes. I encouraged them to move slowly, taking a few minutes to immerse themselves in the environment they were committed to protecting.

When they returned, I asked what the mindfulness walk had been like for them. Several of the board members described elements of the trail and physical surroundings they had never noticed before, including both the natural beauty of the environment and the different ways that people were using the trail. Most notably, the board chair commented during that this was the slowest he had ever moved along the trail, as he would normally jog or bike it solely for the purpose of exercise, and that the mindfulness walk allowed him to really "see" the trail in a new way, and to more deeply appreciate its importance as a community resource. This mindfulness walk and their immediate, in-the-moment experience of the trail allowed the board members to engage with the discussion of the organization's mission statement in a very present, embodied way. This conversation resulted in meaningful updates to the mission and in the creation of a set of values statements that reflected the organization's dedication to both the environment and the local community.

As this example reflects, simple mindfulness practices can be incorporated into organizational meetings, strategic planning sessions, and retreats to support a deeper level of perception and reflection among participants. The research and exercises presented in the rest of this chapter focus on individual-level mindfulness and its relationship to organizational creativity and collaboration.

Theory and Research on Individual-Level Mindfulness in the Workplace

This chapter surveys contemporary research on individual-level mindfulness in the workplace, illustrating how mindfulness and contemplative arts practices can support openness, receptivity, relaxation, well-being, self-awareness, and creativity for those working in organizational contexts. The second part of the chapter introduces specific mindfulness and contemplative arts exercises designed to enhance mindfulness in the workplace on an individual level. The practices introduced in this chapter lay the foundation for the group- and team-level exercises presented in the following chapters. They can be used very effectively as standalone exercises, or to introduce and contextualize the exercises that appear in subsequent chapters.

Much of the research on the benefits of mindfulness, as well as the potential applications of mindfulness to workplace and organizational settings, has focused on the effects of mindfulness practices on the mental, emotional, and physical states of individuals. Indeed, individual-level mindfulness is a basic building block that supports creativity and collaboration on the level of teams and organizations. As described in the Introduction, mindfulness practices can help to foster self-awareness, relaxation, and attention, as well as the creativity-related traits of openness to experience and cognitive flexibility.

As psychologist Dan Siegel (2007, 2010) observed, mindful states of consciousness include both the awareness of one's subjective experience, as well as a sense of openness and receptivity to whatever is occurring interpersonally and in the wider environment on a moment-to-moment basis. Similarly, psychologist Ellen Langer (1989/2014) defined *mindfulness* as "the process of actively noticing new things" (p. 68). The practice of mindfulness allows individuals to become more present themselves and others, and to engage more fully with whatever tasks or activities are calling for their attention in the present moment, including workplace activities. In this way, individual-level mindfulness lays the foundation for the creative process by helping to open up new possibilities and perspectives.

Individual-level mindfulness is also an important component of emotional intelligence, as described by psychologist Daniel Goleman (1995/2005, 2011), of which self-awareness and self-management are important cornerstones. Mindfulness has been demonstrated to correlate with higher levels of emotional intelligence and well-being (Schutte & Malouff, 2011). As Goleman and Lippincott (2017) explained, mindfulness practice can lay the groundwork for the self-awareness needed to deepen emotional intelligence in the workplace, which in turn correlates to better workplace relationships, performance, and productivity.

In my doctoral research study, the co-researchers reported feeling more relaxed, more calm and open, more curious, and more aware of their thoughts and feelings following the mindfulness practices introduced during the workshop sessions. These mindfulness-related traits also increased over time, with each successive meeting. The co-researchers described feeling able to slow down and pay attention to what was occurring for them in the present moment, including their posture, physical sensations, and energy levels. Several also reported a greater sense of self-awareness and openness to ideas after practicing the mindfulness exercises. For example, one person described receiving insight into her own attitude and presence, which gave her a greater sense of choice and consciousness about how she wanted to participate in and contribute to that day's session.

These findings build upon prior psychological literature linking mindfulness to self-awareness and emotional intelligence (Goleman, 1995/2005; Langer, 2014; Siegel, 2007, 2010, 2012). This research also strengthens existing evidence for the connection between mindfulness, creativity, and openness to experience, suggesting that mindfulness practice can lead to greater openness and creativity (Kaufman, 2013; Kaufman & Gregoire, 2015; Kaufman et al., 2016; Shi, Dai, & Lu, 2016; Richards, 2007, 2010).

Mindfulness and Contemplative Arts Exercises for Individual-Level Mindfulness

The exercises presented in this chapter are designed to develop and support individual-level mindfulness in the workplace, including both self-awareness and awareness of the environment. They emphasize present-moment awareness of bodily, physical sensations, emotions, and thoughts, along with opening to the sense perceptions, as described in the traditional Buddhist teachings on the four foundations of mindfulness and contemporary contemplative arts pedagogy. These exercises lay the foundation for the activities that will be described in the following chapters and can be utilized on their own to introduce basic mindfulness practices, or as a lead-in to the exercises presented in later chapters.

As discussed in Chap. 2, mindfulness and contemplative arts exercises can help individuals working in groups to broaden their awareness of both their own internal experiences and what is happening in the world around them, including their physical workspace and the office environment as well as the people and situations around them. The fast pace and urgent deadlines of the contemporary business world, as well as the tendency to multitask, often comes at the cost of our self-awareness and awareness of the wider system and environment in which we are operating. The practices offered here can help deepen self-awareness, relaxation, and openness that are necessary for true organizational creativity, collaboration, and innovation.

A Note on the Structure of the Exercises and the Importance of Debriefing

The practices described in this and the following chapters are presented with a particular structure in mind, which is useful both in learning about the exercises as a facilitator and in presenting them in real-world organizational settings. I first introduce the practice and provide some context for it, then give a set of instructions for guiding the exercise, followed by a set of instructions for debrief and discussion once the exercise has been completed. The true value in these exercises lays in this final step of debriefing and discussion, which is where the real wisdom and insight arises. The debrief and discussion portion of the practice allows participants to reflect upon and share their experiences of the exercise, which often leads to new insight regarding shared experiences and "aha!" moments, allowing group members to harvest the experiential knowledge they have gained from the exercises and to think about how they might apply these insights to their day-to-day work and team experiences.

Guided Mindfulness Practice

The foundational element in this series of exercises is a basic mindfulness meditation practice. There are many wonderful courses, trainings, books, articles, podcasts, and apps that offer guided mindfulness meditation instruction. The version I offer here synthesizes a number of mindfulness meditation instructions I have received over the years in a variety of practice and retreat contexts, including my Buddhist meditation training, my academic education, and my ongoing professional development. I have led this practice in a wide array of group and organizational contexts over the years, and it is designed to be jargon-free and applicable to a variety of organizational contexts.

This guided mindfulness practice is useful for developing individual-level mindfulness, relaxation, and self-awareness, as well as for clearing the mind and transitioning between activities and tasks. This practice can be done anywhere, throughout the day, in just a few minutes. I have found it helpful to begin meetings with a few minutes of mindfulness practice to allow attendees to fully arrive and have a moment of quiet and stillness before the meeting begins, followed by a brief check-in. Groups often find it refreshing to begin meetings this way; it allows people to be more present to the content of the meeting and tends to support a higher quality of participation and information sharing.

Context/Purpose

The purpose of this exercise is to cultivate the ability to be present to ourselves and to our moment-to-moment experience, just as it is, in the moment. This is not about trying to change, improve, or fix anything about ourselves, but more about opening to our experience with a sense of gentleness and curiosity; it's about making friends with ourselves, as meditation teacher Pema Chödrön (1991, 2001, 2013) describes it. We could give ourselves permission to just be and to relax into the experience of being rather than doing. The idea is that we can trust our experience just as it is; we are awake and every moment is fresh. When guiding this exercise, it is important to explain that mindfulness is not always easy or comfortable at first and that there is no "right" or "wrong" way to do it. It is simply about sitting with ourselves and becoming present to our physical sensations, emotions, thoughts, and sense perceptions.

Practice Instructions

We can practice virtually anywhere, simply sitting in a chair, sitting cross-legged on the floor (preferably on a cushion or folded blanket), or even standing. The posture is upright but relaxed, with feet flat on the floor (if sitting on a chair or standing), allowing the natural curves of the spine without either slumping or tensing up. Feel a sense of grounding, with your feet or hips on the floor, allowing the weight of gravity, and sensing your connection to the earth. If sitting, the hands can rest on the thighs, with the neck and jaw relaxed. The eyes can be closed or open with a soft gaze downward. It can be helpful to practice with the eyes open in order to cultivate openness and presence without shutting anything out.

[Pause to allow people to experience the posture of meditation.]

It can be helpful to start with a body scan, or simply by noticing how our bodies are feeling right now, including physical sensations, temperature, areas of tension and relaxation, and so on. We can also open to our sense perceptions, such as the feeling of the air on our skin, the ambient sounds in the room, any scents that we can detect, or lingering tastes in our mouth. Notice the sensation of breathing, including where in the body you feel the breath (nose, chest, abdomen, back, etc.). There is no need to alter or change the breath in any way; simply breathe naturally. The breath is always with us, and it's something we can come back to again and again, in every moment.

[Pause to allow people to experience the feeling of breathing.]

If we notice that our thoughts have carried us away from the present moment (into distractions, the to-do list, or repetitive thought patterns), we can simply bring our attention and awareness back to the body and the breathing. We're not trying to get rid of our thoughts, but simply noticing where our mind goes; thinking is a natural brain activity and an important part of our creative energy. However, if we find our thoughts mind taking us away from our present-moment experience, we can simply come back to the body, to the sensation of breathing, again and again. This is the essence of meditation and mindfulness.

[Pause to let people experience this mindfulness practice and continue in silence for five to ten minutes, occasionally reminding people of the basic instructions around posture, breathing, and working with thoughts.]

Debrief and Discussion

Ask people about their experience of the practice. What did they notice? Was the practice challenging? Did it feel natural? Did they experience particular physical sensations? What did they observe about their mental and emotional states? Their responses will depend in part on their prior familiarity and experience with meditation and mindfulness, as well as their particular present-moment circumstances. It is important to emphasize that there are no right or wrong answers here; the debrief is simply a tool to help participants reflect on their direct experience of the practice and begin to harvest and incorporate any insights.

Once everyone who wishes to speak has shared their experiences of the exercise, ask how they might begin to apply this type of mindfulness practice into their daily work habits and routines. Often people will aspire to take a few minutes of mindfulness practice or even just a few mindful breaths at some point during their workday, perhaps during their lunch break or when feeling particularly stressed. When I recently asked a group of leaders at a major tech company how they might apply or incorporate this practice into their work lives, one participant said she planned to immediately implement a practice of ending meetings five minutes early to allow attendees a little bit of transition time before their next meetings or activities.

Mindful Seeing and Mindfulness Walk

Context/Purpose

The purpose of this exercise is to open our senses, to the world around us, and specifically to our work environment. It is a practice of seeing from a fresh perspective, as Marcel Proust (1923) famously observed, "The real voyage of discovery consists not in seeking new landscapes, but in having new eyes" (as cited by goodreads.com). The demands of our jobs often require a laser focus, along with tight project deadlines and a long list of tasks. The cost of this pressure is that we can lose a sense of perspective and stop seeing what's around us, which can cause us to miss important cues, feedback, and nuances of communication. This exercise is useful for opening our eyes to the world around us, including the details of our everyday experience that we might normally pass over, ignore, take for granted, or not even notice at all. This allows us to see the bigger picture, so that we can begin to cultivate a deeper appreciation for what is, become aware of what's missing or what's needed, and explore tangible changes that could support greater awareness and creativity. This exercise is adapted from several contemplative arts exercises emphasizing mindfulness of the environment and visual perception (as described in McQuade & Hall, 2015; Saitzyk, 2013).

Practice Instructions, Part 1: Mindful Seeing

Ask participants to stand up and find a spot in the room where each person has ample space around them. Invite them to close their eyes and take a few relaxed breaths, feeling the ground beneath their feet. After a few moments, ask them to take a quarter turn to the right, slowly open their eyes, and take in the visual environment in front of them, looking up, down, and straight ahead. Encourage them to actively notice shapes, colors, textures, patterns, light and shadow, and so on, without judgment or evaluation.

Instruct them to pay attention to any thoughts or preferences they notice during this practice (such as "I like this / I don't like this / This is beautiful / This is ugly / This is boring," etc.). Ask them to take a mental image of what they see with their mind's eye for a few moments and then close their eyes again. After a brief pause, ask them to take another quarter turn to the right, and repeat the process, noticing what's in their field of vision, simply taking in the visual environment and observing any thoughts or judgments that arise in connection with the experience. Ask them to again take a mental snapshot of what they see and then close their eyes again. Repeat this process with two more quarter turns until each person has arrived back at their starting position.

At the end of the exercise, invite the participants to take a photo with their camera phones (if they have them handy) of one thing they saw during the exercise that caught their attention` or was particularly striking, vivid, or noteworthy, for later sharing with the group.

Practice Instructions, Part 2: Mindfulness Walk

Invite the group to remain in silence, and to continue the practice of active noticing and attention with a mindful walk around the space; this could be the actual office or meeting space of the gathering, and could also include an outdoor walk. Ask them to take a slow walk (about half the speed of their normal walking pace) around the environment and actively to notice and engage with what they see. Set a timer and ring a bell or gong at the end to bring everyone back to their seats. This could be followed by a brief period of journaling to note what they saw, and/or a group discussion and sharing about their experiences.

Debrief and Discussion

Invite a discussion of what people noticed about the environment and what this experience was like for them. Ask them to describe what they saw during the rotation exercise, what they photographed, and what they noticed during their mindfulness walks. Invite them to share the photo they took at the end of the mindful seeing exercise. Often participants will note seeing a familiar, everyday environment in a new way, including objects, artwork, or features of the landscape they have never noticed before or simply took for granted.

Follow-Up Questions and Integration

In order to deepen the experience and allow participants to begin integrating and applying it to their workplace activities, pose the following questions and note the responses.

- What are you not noticing or taking for granted about your job, your team, your organization?
- What if we took the time to really see what and who is around us at work?
- What might we do differently?

- How might it change our work relationships, collaboration, creativity, and productivity?

When I led this exercise during a creativity meetup group, it sparked a deep discussion into the nature of art itself and spurred some very interesting reflections on how the participants, working in different creative fields and mediums, might go about their creative work in a new way and approach their creative process with fresh eyes.

Somatic Awareness Exercise

Context/Purpose
The purpose of this exercise is to give participants a chance to deepen their experience of mindfulness and ground it into their physical experience with somatic awareness. Often we hold tension and stress in our bodies that we are largely unaware of on a conscious level, and this holding can greatly affect our day-to-day experience of our work. Our physical bodies also contain tremendous wisdom that we can tap into for greater creativity and insight.

Practice Instructions
This somatic awareness exercise involves an exploration of individual-level mindfulness of body using movement and gesture. Ask each person to find a spot in the room where they have a bit of space around them to move freely without bumping into anyone else. This exercise can be done with each person facing away from the others, toward a wall, or at least done with eyes closed (this is not a performance for anyone else to see, but rather a personal exploration).

Ask each participant to make a gesture, take a posture, or find a movement that represents and embodies how they are feeling about a particular work-related or creative challenge. Invite them to really get curious about this physical gesture or movement and pay close attention to how it feels in the body, noticing any physical sensations, feelings, and/or emotions that go along with it. Once they have explored and settled on a particular gesture or posture, ask them to hold it for a few moments, like a statue.

Then invite them to transition to a new gesture that embodies how they *want* to feel with respect to this challenge, to explore what it would feel like if they could find their way through the challenge to a satisfying solution. Once they have each settled on a particular gesture or posture, ask them to again hold it for a few moments and notice the physical sensations, feelings, and emotions that go along with it. Ask them what's possible here, in this new space, that wasn't before. How does it feel different? What are they noticing?

Debrief and Discussion

Upon completion of the exercise, allow participants a moment of transition, perhaps inviting them to take a few breaths and then ask them to slowly open their eyes and return to their seats. Ask about their experience of the exercise, what they noticed while doing it, and how it felt in their bodies, including physical sensations, thoughts, emotions, and so on. Ask if any particular insights emerged during or after the exercise.

People often remark that their initial posture felt tense and tight, that they noticed physical tension and/or a feeling of constriction in their bodies, and that the second posture felt more open, more spacious, and expansive. There are no right or wrong answers here; this is simply an exercise of exploration and noticing.

Follow-Up Questions and Applications

- How could you apply this new level of somatic awareness to the actual work-related challenge you identified?
- Is there anything new you could try or anything you could do differently in your day-to-day work by operating from this space?

Summary

The research and exercises presented in this chapter focused on individual-level mindfulness and its relevance to workplace creativity, integrating theoretical perspectives and experiential practice of mindfulness meditation practice, mindful seeing, and somatic awareness. These basic practices provide the context and foundation for the research, mindfulness, and contemplative arts practices described in the following chapters. Chapter 5 presents research and exercises related to trust and authentic communication in organizational teams.

References

Chödrön, P. (1991). *The wisdom of no escape and the path of loving-kindness.* Boston, MA: Shambhala Publications.

Chödrön, P. (2001). *The places that scare you: A guide to fearlessness in difficult times.* Boston, MA: Shambhala Publications.

Chödrön, P. (2013). *How to meditate: A practical guide to making friends with your mind.* Lewisville, CO: Sounds True.

Goleman, D. (1995/2005). *Emotional intelligence: Why it can matter more than IQ* (10th anniversary ed.). New York, NY: Bantam Books.

Goleman, D. (2011). *Leadership: The power of emotional intelligence.* Florence, MA: More Than Sound.

Goleman, D., & Lippincott, M. (2017). Without emotional intelligence, mindfulness doesn't work. *Harvard Business Review.* Retrieved from https://hbr.org/2017/09/sgc-what-really-makes-mindfulness-work

Kaufman, S. B. (2013). Opening up openness to experience: A four-factor model and relations to creative achievement in the arts and sciences. *The Journal of Creative Behavior, 47*(4), 233–255. https://doi.org/10.1002/jocb.33

Kaufman, S. B., & Gregoire, C. (2015). *Wired to create: Unraveling the mysteries of the creative mind.* New York, NY: Perigee.

Kaufman, S. B., Quilty, L. C., Grazioplene, R. G., Hirsh, J. B., Gray, J. R., Peterson, J. B., & DeYoung, C. G. (2016). Openness to experience and intellect differentially predict creative achievement in the arts and sciences. *Journal of Personality, 84*(2), 248–258. https://doi.org/10.1111/jopy.12156

Langer, E. (1989/2014). *Mindfulness* (25th anniversary ed.). Boston, MA: Da Capo Press.

Langer, E. (2014, March). Mindfulness in the age of complexity. *Harvard Business Review*, pp. 68–73. Retrieved from https://hbr.org/2014/03/mindfulness-in-the-age-of-complexity

McQuade, J., & Hall, M. (2015). *Looking and seeing: Nalanda Miksang contemplative photography.* Madison, WI: Drala Publishing.

Proust, M. (1923). *La Prisonniere.* Quote retrieved from https://www.goodreads.com/quotes/33702-the-real-voyage-of-discovery-consists-not-in-seeking-new

Richards, R. (Ed.). (2007). *Everyday creativity and new views of human nature: Psychological, social, and spiritual perspectives.* Washington, DC: American Psychological Association.

Richards, R. (2010). Everyday creativity: Process and way of life—Four key issues. In J. C. Kaufman & R. J. Sternberg (Eds.), *The Cambridge handbook of creativity* (pp. 189–215). New York, NY: Cambridge University Press.

Saitzyk, S. (2013). *Place your thoughts here: Meditation for the creative mind.* Los Angeles, CA: First Thought Press.

Schutte, N. S., & Malouff, J. M. (2011). Emotional intelligence mediates the relationship between mindfulness and subjective well-being. *Personality and Individual Differences, 50*(7), 1116–1119.

Shi, B., Dai, D. Y., & Lu, Y. (2016, May). Openness to experience as a moderator of the relationship between intelligence and creative thinking: A study of Chinese children in urban and rural areas. *Frontiers in Psychology, 7*, 641. https://doi.org/10.3389/fpsyg.2016.00641

Siegel, D. (2007). *The mindful brain: Reflection and attunement in the cultivation of well-being*. New York, NY: W. W. Norton & Co.

Siegel, D. (2010). *The mindful therapist: A clinician's guide to mindsight and neural integration*. New York, NY: W. W. Norton & Co.

Siegel, D. (2012). *The developing mind: How relationships and the brain interact to shape who we are*. New York, NY: The Guilford Press.

CHAPTER 5

Establishing Trust and Authentic Communication Among Organizational Teams

Abstract This chapter surveys contemporary research on psychological safety, trust, and communication, discussing how these interpersonal, affective elements of the team experience relate to team collaboration and productivity. It then describes how mindfulness and contemplative arts practices can help to foster a sense of trust and open communication among members of a team. With this research and context in mind, the second part of the chapter lays out specific mindfulness and contemplative arts exercises designed to help foster the sense of safety and trust among teams and groups that is vital for open communication and dialogue.

Keywords Trust • Communication • Teams • Psychological safety • Collaboration

Building Empathy and Trust Through Mindful Speaking and Listening

One of the most powerful exercises I have experienced and witnessed over the years in many different contexts, from intensive meditation retreats to the Search Inside Yourself Leadership Institute's mindful leadership training (developed at Google), is the practice of active, empathic listening within the context of a structured dyad. Time and time again I have noted

M. J. Rothouse, *A Mindful Approach to Team Creativity and Collaboration in Organizations*, Palgrave Studies in Creativity and Innovation in Organizations,
https://doi.org/10.1007/978-3-030-47675-5_5

the profound impact of simply bearing witness to another person's experience without judgment or response, and of being witnessed in this way, whether with someone I already know or (sometimes even more powerfully) with a complete stranger, for after practicing this exercise, the stranger is a stranger no more. A very simple and straightforward, yet deep, sense of empathy and connection develops naturally from this practice, even after only five minutes with someone you've just met.

In a structured dyad (described in more precise detail and presented as an exercise later in this chapter), one takes turns acting as both speaker and listener. When speaking, there is no dialogue or response from the listener; you have the opportunity to share something that is in your mind or heart, and to simply be heard and witnessed. When listening, your only role is to listen without responding, without agenda, simply opening your being to receive what the speaker is communicating. In the beginning, it may feel a little bit awkward and self-conscious to share in this way; some people feel more comfortable listening than sharing and vice versa, particularly with people they don't know well. Indeed, how often in daily life are we able to simply share something authentic about ourselves and our experience with another person for no "purpose" or intended result? Over time, the practice begins to feel more and more natural, often leading to deepening connections and lasting friendships.

With practice, it feels easier to share openly and to be vulnerable with someone who is simply holding space for you. As a listener, one learns what a gift it is to give another person your full attention and presence, without responding, merely holding space for their experience. It can be difficult at first not to react or respond, but people often begin to experience their own empathy at hearing others' stories and it helps them to feel more connected.

I have practiced this kind of active listening in many different contexts, both professional and personal, and have found it an incredibly useful tool for approaching difficult conversations, working through misunderstandings and conflict, and deepening important relationships. I believe that listening is an underrated superpower, one that is incredibly important for developing trust and connection, particularly for those working as organizational leaders, coaches, and facilitators. The research and exercises presented in this chapter thus focus on the importance of empathy, trust, psychological safety, and authentic communication among organizational teams, as well as how cultivating these qualities can support workplace creativity and collaboration.

Theory and Research on Empathy, Trust, and Communication in Teams

This chapter surveys contemporary research on psychological safety, trust, and communication, discussing how these interpersonal, affective elements of the team experience relate to team collaboration and productivity. It then describes how mindfulness and contemplative arts practices can help to foster a sense of trust and open communication among members of a team. With this research and context in mind, the second part of the chapter lays out specific mindfulness and contemplative arts exercises designed to help foster the sense of safety and trust among teams and groups that is vital for open communication and dialogue.

Because group creativity and collaboration require the cooperation of several (or many) people working together toward a common vision and goals, it is essential that they share a sense of trust, open communication, and positive working relationships, as well as a shared sense of interdependence and a belief in the potential benefits of collaboration (Alencar, 2012; Boucher, 2014; Giles, Denes, Hamilton, & Hajda, 2009; Hess von Ludewig, 2014; John-Steiner, 2000, 2011; Miyashiro, 2011; Sawyer & DeZutter, 2009). In a study of organizational decision making and team collaboration, Ejamabo (2015) identified communication and trust as vital for both effective leadership and teamwork. Similarly, Google's internal research on team effectiveness (Duhigg, 2016; Rozovsky, 2015), emphasized the critical importance of psychological safety and trust for team collaboration. Similarly, Brené Brown's extensive research into leadership and the barriers to open, creative organizational cultures indicated that a lack of empathy and connection among teams and organizations diminishes trust and prevents them from performing at their best (Brown, 2018).

Trust and communication among teams requires a strong foundation of empathy, emotional intelligence, and mindfulness. In her book *The Empathy Factor*, which built upon the principles of non-violent communication (Rosenberg, 2003), Marie Miyashiro (2011) focused on empathy and communication in the workplace. She emphasized how empathy in organizational settings occurs at several levels, including individuals' attuning to their own feelings and emotions, as well as to those of their colleagues, and to the organization as a whole. This type of attunement closely mirrors the four cornerstones of emotional intelligence outlined by Goleman (1995/2005, 2011), including self-awareness, self-management, social awareness, and relationship management.

Another important element of trust and communication is the ability to truly listen, both to oneself and to others. In his work on leadership and organizational effectiveness, MIT professor and leadership scholar Otto Scharmer has observed that effective leadership has a lot to do with attention, and specifically with the ability to listen. Scharmer (2018) has identified four levels of listening, ranging from the most superficial to the deepest: (1) Downloading or listening to confirm what we already know; (2) Factual listening or listening for new information; (3) Empathic listening, in which we actually put ourselves in another person's shoes; and (4) Generative listening, which is transformative for both the speaker and the listener. Most people generally operate from a space of downloading or factual listening, but true creativity and innovation require more empathic and generative listening. Listening in this way allows us to understand the people we work with, and the contexts we're working within, as they are rather than through the lens of our own projections, labels, and judgments. This, in turn, opens up new possibilities for creativity and collaboration. The exercises presented at the end of this chapter focus on developing this level of listening and attunement skills.

My doctoral research further demonstrated how mindfulness and contemplative arts practices can help to build a sense of trust and communication among organizational teams and working groups. Indeed, at the outset of my research process, one of the co-researchers (a co-founder of the organization) noted the importance of honest, open communication between team members, observing that "lack of trust harms creativity and innovation and can create conflict" (Rothouse, 2018). While this may seem obvious, many organizational leaders lack the interpersonal skills needed to foster trust and open communication, and may unwittingly hinder it with their own poor communication skills coupled with an authoritarian or ego-based approach.

In my dissertation research study (Rothouse, 2018), as the co-researchers developed individual-level mindfulness (described in Chap. 3) and then a sense of psychological safety and trust, the quality of communication among the group amplified. Indeed, the co-researchers also noted that participating in the mindfulness and contemplative arts activities allowed them to relax with one another and interact in a way that felt more authentic and open. The contemplative arts process thus helped to foster greater openness, dialogue, and the exchange of ideas along with an appreciation of the differences between, and value of, each other's perspectives, communication styles, and contributions to the ongoing discussions about the future of the organization. The sense of safety and trust that developed among the group increased over time, with the mindfulness and contemplative arts exercises that we practiced from week to week. Gradually, this deepening of trust and open communication paved the way for a greater degree of creative collaboration among the group.

It is important to note that the mindfulness and contemplative arts exercises did not always come easily or naturally to all of the participants, some of whom experienced self-consciousness, as well as a sense of awkwardness and vulnerability when engaging in the activities. This is a very natural response, especially for those who are unfamiliar with mindfulness and meditation practices, who tend toward introversion, or who may feel shy about their own creativity and artistic skill. Thus it is very important for the facilitator to discern the group's comfort level with these kinds of practices, and to design, curate, and contextualize the activities accordingly.

That said, sometimes moving beyond one's comfort zone, in a safe and supportive environment, can lead to insight and growth. In my study, one of the co-researchers described her experience of the mindfulness and contemplative arts exercises as a journey of "getting past my own stuff" (Rothouse, 2018). Others noted that despite (or even because of) the discomfort and vulnerability they felt while participating in the exercises, the experience actually helped them to communicate with their colleagues more authentically. One of the deepest insights for me from this research process was precisely the connection between participants' initial feelings of discomfort or vulnerability and the deepening of the conversations that were possible in the wake of that discomfort. As one of the co-researchers astutely remarked, "I think some of our better conversations, deeper conversations, came out of the activities that I was actually more uncomfortable doing" (Rothouse, 2018). To this point, the poet and organizational leadership consultant David Whyte observed: "life is a creative, intimate, and unpredictable conversation if nothing else, spoken or unspoken, and our life and our work are both the result of the particular way we hold that passionate conversation" (Whyte, 2001, p. 5). Indeed, the willingness to enter into dialogue, even (and particularly) when it is difficult or uncomfortable, is one of the hallmarks of a high-functioning team.

As in many organizations, one of the biggest barriers to authentic communication in my research study was the fear of addressing problematic issues and dynamics. This hesitation was palpable at times, and certain members of the group sensed that others were holding back from expressing their genuine thoughts and feelings. Once this was acknowledged, some expressed frustration and uncertainty about what the group was trying to accomplish together. Indeed, both a hesitation or unwillingness to have the difficult conversations and a lack of clarity around goals and values are among the top barriers to organizational effectiveness, according to Brené Brown (2018).

Another factor that one of the co-researchers expressed was a sense of uncertainty about how her own needs aligned with the priorities of the organization. This feeling of disconnect actually deepened as the research and organizational transition process continued, to the point where she sought out and accepted a position at another organization, which in my view was a healthy and empowering decision for her. This example demonstrates how group processes rooted in mindfulness can actually help individual team members and organizations identify the culture and values they are actually manifesting, as opposed to their stated ideals, allowing for a better sense of either alignment (or disconnect), which can in turn lead to important decisions about team composition.

Another challenge that the co-researchers observed with respect to the mindfulness and contemplative arts process was a lack of coherence between the experiences of relaxation, openness, and collaboration they felt during the exercises and the challenging conversations that needed to happen about the organizational culture and business decisions. Indeed, as described above, some expressed frustration that others were holding back, particularly early on in the process. Once this frustration had been named, along with the increasing feelings of trust and safety that developed during the workshop process, the group was able to achieve a more authentic level of dialogue and discussion, including a sense of "radical honesty," as one of the organizational co-founders described it (Rothouse, 2018).

Mindfulness and Contemplative Arts Exercises for Empathy, Trust, Psychological Safety, and Communication

The exercises presented in this section build upon the individual-level mindfulness exercises presented in the previous chapter to develop mindfulness of self and other while facilitating trust, psychological safety, and open communication between individuals and among groups. The major focus of these activities is on cultivating empathy, connection, and attunement among members of teams and workgroups.

Mindful Speaking and Listening Exercise

Context/Purpose

The purpose of this exercise is to allow participants to practice mindful speaking, listening, and witnessing, which are important skills for building emotional intelligence, empathy, trust, and communication. The exercise takes place in structured dyads, helping to develop skills of authentic communication and empathic listening. While much of contemporary work life involves communication in various forms (face to face, phone, videoconferencing, email, and text), we rarely listen to others in an active, empathic way, without agenda and without thinking about how we will respond. Listening is an art, and it can be an incredibly profound and compassionate act if done skillfully. And conversely, how often are we truly able to speak about something important to us in our work life and simply feel heard, with another person's full attention and presence? Listening is hugely vital for creativity and collaboration in the workplace, as well as for effective leadership of creative teams, and it's something everyone can improve upon.

Practice Instructions, Part 1

Beginning with a few minutes of mindfulness practice, as described in Chap. 4, or by simply taking a few breaths in silence, ask participants to break into pairs for a practice of mindful speaking and listening in structured dyads. Emphasize that this is a practice of authentic, heart-based sharing and witnessing, and that anything shared within the exercise should remain confidential. The facilitator should time the exercise, giving each speaker two to five minutes to speak, depending on time constraints. Ask each pair to designate who will speak and who will listen first.

Once each pair has designated a speaker and listener, ask the speakers to verbally share something about either a current creative project or challenge they are facing in their organizational role. The facilitator should start the timer and ring a gong or chime to begin and end the exercise. During this time, the speaker has the floor and the listener should only listen, with their full presence, without reacting, responding, interjecting, or crosstalk, to what the speaker is saying. If the speaker runs out of things to say, the pair can simply sit in silence without further discussion or chatter until the facilitator concludes this portion of the exercise.

Once the time is up, invite each pair to return to a few moments of mindful breathing in silence. Then, ask the pair to switch roles, so that the speaker becomes the listener and vice versa. Repeat the instructions above, ringing a gong or chime to signal the end of the exercise, and then invite the pair to return again to mindful breathing, taking a few moments to reflect upon what this experience was like for them, including both the speaking and listening portions. Depending on time constraints, the exercise could conclude here or extend to Part 2.

Practice Instructions, Part 2

Allow each pair an opportunity to debrief with one another, again in structured, timed dyads. Each listener will have the opportunity to share both what they heard from the speaker and what the experience was like for them. Allow two to three minutes for this portion for each member of the pair, with each listener in turn sharing first what they heard their partner say and then what they experienced, including any physical sensations, emotions, or thoughts that accompanied the experience of listening. This is not about responding to what the speaker said, or about giving advice or dialogue, and again there should be no crosstalk or discussion. This is simply an opportunity for each person to share what they heard and experienced as a listener, and to describe their experience of witnessing the other person. Once each person has shared their experience of listening, ask the pairs to thank each other and return to the larger group.

Debrief and Discussion

Ask participants to share what it was like for them to play each role—that of both speaker and listener—including what they noticed in their physical bodies, emotions, and thoughts.

- What was it like to simply be heard and witnessed in this way?
- What was it like to speak without receiving an immediate response?
- What was it like to listen without responding?
- What did they notice about this experience and what it might be like to both listen to and be heard by their colleagues in this way in the context of their day-to-day work or organizational role?

- How might they incorporate this kind of mindful speaking and listening into their work and personal lives?

Mirroring Exercise

Context/Purpose

Mirroring is a popular exercise in both dance and movement therapy (DMT) and improvisational theater circles, and there are many different versions of this exercise widely available. The purpose of the exercise is to develop attunement and empathy, which in turn leads to a greater sense of trust and safety. Researchers and practitioners of dance and movement therapy describe the power of mirroring to allow people to experience feeling seen and witnessed on a deep, somatic level (Hart, 2008; Stromsted, 2009). According to McGarry and Russo (2011), mirroring engages the mirror neuron system of the brain, which is important in activating empathy. Indeed, as Harvey (1994) explained, once safety and attunement have been established using this type of exercise, true creativity can emerge.

Practice Instructions

The version offered here is a synthesis of my experience with this exercise in the context of several different classes and workshops over the years. The exercise is done in pairs and, as in the practice of mindful speaking and listening, each member of the pair will have the opportunity to play the role of both mover and mirror. Once the instructions are given by the facilitator, this exercise should be practiced in silence. The facilitator should act as timekeeper, signaling the beginning and end of each phase of the exercise.

Ask participants to divide into pairs, with each pair finding a space in the room where they can engage in the exercise without distraction. Ask each pair to designate a mover and a mirror. The mover will begin a series of simple physical movements and gestures, beginning with facial expressions or hand gestures, and the mirror will simply mimic their movements, paying close attention to what the mover is doing and following along with their own body as though they are a mirror. This will require a great deal of focus and attention on the mover. The mover should be sure to keep their movements simple enough that the mirror can easily follow along. Continue for a timed period of two to three minutes, with each pair returning to silence and taking a few mindful breaths.

After a brief pause, ask the pairs to switch roles, so that the mover becomes the mirror and vice versa. Repeat the instructions and again time the exercise for two to three minutes, bringing the practice to a close with the ring of a gong, chime, or timer. An additional phase of the exercise (if time allows) involves asking the pairs to exchange roles on their own, without prompting from the facilitator and without words, requiring an even deeper level of attunement and non-verbal communication.

Debrief and Discussion

Ask participants to reflect on their experience of the exercise, including what it was like to participate both as the mover and the mirror. The pairs could remain together initially to discuss their experiences together, one-on-one, before rejoining their peers for a group discussion. Ask what people noticed about the experience of playing each role, and what it felt like both to witness and mirror their partner and to be witnessed and mirrored. While some may initially feel self-conscious while doing this exercise, particularly those who have less experience or familiarity with somatic work, often people describe a feeling of resonance and flow, as though the mirror could almost anticipate what the mover would do next. Following this discussion of the experience itself, ask the participants how this exercise might translate into their day-to-day roles on the team and group creative collaboration.

Systems Awareness Exercise

Context/Purpose

The purpose of this exercise is to build upon individual-level mindfulness and to cultivate self-awareness, awareness of others, and awareness of the wider system in which they are operating. This is a full-group activity that allows participants to move together within a defined space while attuning to group dynamics.

Practice Instructions

This exercise requires some open space for people to move around. It may be necessary to move chairs and tables so that there is room for everyone to move freely through the space. Ask participants to spread out and find a spot in the room, facing in any direction. Begin with a few moments of mindfulness practice or mindful breathing. Then ask them to begin moving around the room, in silence, at a normal walking pace in any direction, like particles moving through space. Ask them to maintain awareness of both their own bodies and of the other people in the room, so they don't bump into anyone else.

Continue this way for several minutes, and then ask them to double their speed, maintaining their awareness in order to avoid collisions, and notice how it feels to be moving more quickly through the space. After a few minutes of this, ask people to slow down to half speed, so that everyone is moving in slow motion, continuing to pay attention to the breath, to physical sensations, emotions, and thoughts. Finally, ask them to come to a stop and stand in place, return to mindful breathing, and simply take a moment to experience the stillness. Then bring the exercise to a close and invite them to return to their seats.

Debrief and Discussion

Ask participants to reflect on what it was like to do this exercise, and what they noticed while doing it.

- What was it like to move at each different pace within the group?
- What physical, emotional, and mental states did they experience during each portion of the exercise?
- What aspect of the exercise felt most comfortable for them? Least comfortable?
- What insights, if any, emerged with respect to their self-awareness and awareness of the group/system in which they were participating?
- How might this experience inform their work within their team or organization?

When I led this exercise with a group of emerging leaders at a major tech company, during the debrief some observed that moving faster felt easier or more familiar, but also more reactive, while some expressed that moving more slowly felt less comfortable but also more deliberate or intentional. This speaks to the speed at which many organizations operate, and invites the question of what may be possible in slowing down. How could slowing down in the work environment allow for more intention and less reactivity? When I asked how they might carry this insight forward in their work, one person said it helped her to better see how she may be contributing to certain negative workplace dynamics and allow her to make different choices, which demonstrated her growing self-awareness.

Summary

The research and exercises presented in this chapter focused on the interpersonal aspects of trust and communication among teams and their importance for creativity and collaboration. The chapter surveyed contemporary research related to trust and communication, including psychological safety, empathy, emotional intelligence, listening, and attunement. With this research basis in mind, the mindfulness exercises described in the second part of the chapter focused on developing the skills of listening, attunement, and systems awareness among workgroups and teams. The following chapter, Chap. 6, builds upon the research and exercises described thus far, focusing on team cohesion and collaboration.

References

Alencar, E. M. L. S. (2012). Creativity in organizations: Facilitators and inhibitors. In M. Mumford (Ed.), *Handbook of organizational creativity* (pp. 87–111). San Diego, CA: Academic Press.

Boucher, R. H. (2014). *Creative breakthrough emergence: A conversational accomplishment* (Doctoral dissertation). Retrieved from ProQuest Dissertations and Theses (UMI No: 3642065).

Brown, B. (2018). *Dare to lead: Brave work, tough conversations, whole hearts.* London, UK: Vermillion.

Duhigg, C. (2016, February 25). What Google learned from its quest to build a perfect team. *The New York Times Magazine.* Retrieved from www.nytimes.com/2016/02/28/magazine/what-google-learned-from-its-quest-to-build-the-perfect-team.html

Ejamabo, N. O. (2015). The influence of decision making in organizational leadership and management activities. *Journal of Entrepreneurship and Organization Management, 4*(2). https://doi.org/10.4172/2169-026X.1000138

Giles, H., Denes, A., Hamilton, D. L., & Hajda, J. M. (2009). Striking a chord: A prelude to music and intergroup relations research. *Group Processes & Intergroup Relations, 12*(3), 291–301.

Goleman, D. (1995/2005). *Emotional intelligence: Why it can matter more than IQ* (10th anniversary ed.). New York, NY: Bantam Books.

Goleman, D. (2011). *Leadership: The power of emotional intelligence.* Florence, MA: More Than Sound.

Hart, S. (2008). *Brain, attachment, personality: An introduction to neuro-affective development.* London, UK: Karnac.

Harvey, S. (1994). Dynamic play therapy: An integrated expressive arts approach to the family treatment of infants and toddlers. *Zero to Three, 15*(1), 11–18.

Hess von Ludewig, H. K. (2014). *Networked creativity: Understanding the process and effect of interpersonal and networked interactions on workplace creativity* (Doctoral dissertation). Retrieved from ProQuest Dissertations and Theses (UMI No: 3647627).

John-Steiner, V. (2000). *Creative collaboration.* New York, NY: Oxford University Press.

John-Steiner, V. (2011). Collaboration. In M. Runco & S. Pritzker (Eds.), *Encyclopedia of creativity* (2nd ed., pp. 222–225). San Diego, CA: Academic Press.

McGarry, L. M., & Russo, F. A. (2011). Mirroring in dance/movement therapy: Potential mechanisms behind empathy enhancement. *The Arts in Psychotherapy, 38*(3), 178–184.

Miyashiro, M. R. (2011). *The empathy factor: Your competitive advantage for personal, team, and business success.* Encinitas, CA: Puddle Jumper Press.

Rosenberg, M. B. (2003). *Nonviolent communication: A language of life.* Encinitas, CA: PuddleDancer Press.

Rothouse, M. (2018). *Facilitating team creativity and collaboration using mindfulness and contemplative arts* (Doctoral dissertation). Retrieved from ProQuest Dissertations and Theses (Order No. 10823776).

Rozovsky, J. (2015, November 17). The five keys to a successful Google team. Retrieved from https://rework.withgoogle.com/blog/five-keys-to-a-successful-google-team/

Sawyer, R. K., & DeZutter, S. (2009). Distributed creativity: How collective creations emerge from collaboration. *Psychology of Aesthetics, Creativity and the Arts, 3*(2), 81–92.

Scharmer, O. (2018). Leading from the future: A new social technology for our times. Retrieved from https://thesystemsthinker.com/leading-from-the-future-a-new-social-technology-for-our-times/

Stromsted, T. (2009). Authentic movement: A dance with the divine. *Body, Movement and Dance in Psychotherapy Journal, 4,* 201–213.

Whyte, D. (2001). *Crossing the unknown sea: Work as a pilgrimage of identity.* New York, NY: Riverhead Books.

CHAPTER 6

Facilitating Team Cohesion and Collaboration

Abstract This chapter examines relevant research and scholarship on team cohesion and collaboration, describing how mindfulness and contemplative arts practices can help teams to coalesce and work together meaningfully toward creative and organizational goals. It then offers a series of exercises and activities that facilitators can use to support team cohesion and collaboration in the context of learning and development trainings, workshops, and organizational retreats.

Keywords Team cohesion • Collaboration • Mindfulness • Contemplative arts • Creativity

Sonic Meditations and the Power of Resonance

One of the most powerful contemplative arts exercises I have experienced over the years, and one I have led with many different groups in many different contexts, is the sonic meditation, based on Pauline Oliveros' work with musical improvisation, mindfulness, and deep listening. I first experienced the practice of sonic meditation, led by Lance Brunner, during a contemplative arts retreat (described at the beginning of Chap. 3).

M. J. Rothouse, *A Mindful Approach to Team Creativity and Collaboration in Organizations*, Palgrave Studies in Creativity and Innovation in Organizations,
https://doi.org/10.1007/978-3-030-47675-5_6

In *The Sonic Meditations*, Oliveros (1974) articulated a process of group sound improvisation based on the principles of deep listening and non-judgmental awareness, which involves simply creating sound using the voice and body, while sitting in a circle with eyes closed. It's not about making beautiful sounds, but simply listening, responding, and offering sound into the circle, in connection with others. Every time I experience or lead this exercise, I am reminded of the magic of improvisation and how each instance of the sonic meditations is completely unique depending on the group of people assembled, the setting, and the context. Yet in each instance, the group naturally settles into a collective rhythm, finding resonance and playfulness while creating a sonic tapestry together.

The first time I experienced it, the exercise felt both meditative and playful, reminding me of the power of resonance I had experienced years earlier singing a cappella in college, blending and harmonizing voices, and the powerful feeling of attunement it creates. In the intervening years, I went on to lead this exercise with many different groups in a variety of settings, ranging in number from just a handful of people up to 20 or 30 or more. The groups included both existing teams who were already well acquainted with one another and individuals who met for the first time in the context of a creativity workshop or class. Participation in this exercise became a turning point in the team dynamics in my dissertation research study, allowing the group to coalesce more powerfully, as I describe below. It is truly one of the most powerful tools I have experienced for facilitating group cohesion and collaboration, and I have included instructions for leading it as part of this chapter.

Theory and Research on Team Cohesion and Collaboration

The first section of this chapter examines relevant research and scholarship on team cohesion and collaboration, describing how mindfulness and contemplative arts practices can help teams to coalesce and work together meaningfully toward creative and organizational goals. The second part of the chapter offers a series of exercises and activities that facilitators can use to support team cohesion and collaboration in the context of learning and development trainings, workshops, and organizational retreats.

According to creativity researcher Keith Sawyer (2017), who has spent his career studying the process of group creative collaboration and improvisation, "collaboration is the secret to breakthrough creativity" (p. ix). Sawyer argues that innovation, particularly in organizations, is driven by collaboration. A review of existing literature on team cohesion and collaboration indicates a number of factors that can either enhance or inhibit creative collaboration. As discussed in the previous chapter, collaboration among teams requires a strong degree of trust and communication that allows for individual team members to work together toward common goals. Such collaboration also requires a high degree of cooperation, good working relationships, and a sense of interdependence among the team members (Boucher, 2014; Giles, Denes, Hamilton, & Hajda, 2009; Hess von Ludewig, 2014; John-Steiner, 2000, 2011). For a team to coalesce, each member must transcend their individual perspectives to some extent in order to fully enter into a creative synergy with others (John-Steiner, 2000, 2011).

My doctoral research (Rothouse, 2018) also highlighted the importance for teams to have a sense of clarity and focus with respect to both specific goals and avenues for collaboration (also emphasized by Marlow, Lacerenza, Woods, & Salas, 2018), as well as an understanding how each individual's values, aspirations, and contributions relate to the overall team, project, and organizational goals and vision. These findings echo Google's research into what makes effective teams, which emphasized the necessity of structure, clarity, meaning, and impact, which build upon the more fundamental elements of psychological safety and dependability (Duhigg, 2016; Rozovsky, 2015). My research findings on team cohesion and collaboration also affirm the results of prior research on how mindfulness and arts activities can support feelings of group connection and collaboration (Byrne, 2017; Holm, 2014; Serifsoy, 2012; Smith, 2014).

Mindfulness practices have proven useful in facilitating both team cohesion and creative collaboration. Investigating the links between mindfulness and creativity, Cleirigh and Greaney (2014) found that in randomized teams of students, a brief mindfulness protocol resulted in higher levels of both group cohesion and performance. Similarly, a recent dissertation investigating the effects of a mindfulness training program on creativity in a functional organizational setting indicated increases in individual creativity as well as workgroup creativity and cohesion, using several measures of individual and group creativity (Byrne, 2017).

Arts-based practices—including multimodal expressive arts and improvisation including visual art, movement and dance, music and sound, and theatrical improv—can help to shift individuals' self-awareness and help foster collaboration in a variety of group and organizational contexts (Levine & Levine, 2011; Rogers, 1993, 2011). Specifically, researchers working in the fields of dance and movement therapy have described the effects of movement practices on collaboration in group settings (Adler, 1999, 2002; Chodorow, 1991; Halprin, 1999, 2003; Homann, 2010; Serlin, 1993; Stromsted, 2009; Whitehouse, 1999), while others have utilized techniques of musical and theatrical improvisation to support group collaboration (Galbraith, Subrin, & Ross, 2008; Leonard & Yorton, 2015; Oliveros, 1974; Osborne, 2000; Sawyer, 2017; Smith, 2014; Vera & Crossan, 2005). As described in the introduction to this chapter, Oliveros' work with group musical improvisation emphasized mindfulness, deep listening, and non-judgmental awareness to help develop group cohesion and collaboration and even to facilitate social change (O'Brien, 2016; Oliveros, 1974; Osborne, 2000).

Elements of improvisation from theater and comedy are also being introduced into organizations to support team creativity and collaboration, as described by Leonard and Yorton (2015), leaders of the famed Second City theater in Chicago. They explained how improv principles of "yes, and" (always saying yes to whatever is occurring and building upon it rather than resisting or saying no), active listening, co-creating, innovating from a completely blank slate, and welcoming failure as part of the creative process, can support organizational creativity and innovation (Leonard & Yorton, 2015). Drawing an explicit connection between this type of theatrical improvisation and the kinds of creative collaboration that take place among high-functioning organizational teams, Sawyer (2017) observed:

> In both an improv group and a successful work team, the members play off one another, each person's contributions providing the spark for the next. Together, the improvisational team creates a novel emergent product, one that's more responsive to the changing environment and better than what anyone could have developed alone. (p. 17)

Theatrical improv games require a good deal of mindful attention, self-awareness, receptivity, and awareness of the larger group dynamic, requiring participants to be fully present, open, and accepting of whatever is happening in the field in a process of spontaneous co-creation.

Mindfulness and contemplative arts exercises can also help to reveal where cohesion and collaboration are lacking or have not yet fully flowered among new and existing teams, as my own research revealed. The members of the organizational group that I partnered with on one hand expressed a shared desire to collaborate, yet also initially expressed a sense of confusion around goals and a lack of clarity about the manner of their intended collaboration (Rothouse, 2018). This suggests that although team members may possess a common wish to collaborate, if the methods and objectives for cooperation are unclear, the collaborative process may never materialize. In the case of the co-researchers I worked with, once the group was able to coalesce around a common vision and set of values, their collaboration was able to take root more fully. This finding affirms earlier research by West (1995) asserting the importance of a shared vision and values for group creativity in organizations.

One very revealing insight regarding a lack of cohesion among the group in my research study came about as a result of the movement and gesture exercise that we did together during the third working session. When invited to contribute a gesture to a collaborative group sculpture, some participated playfully and joyfully, while others hesitated or held back from adding their individual gestures, illustrating a lack of cohesion among the full group. This experience proved very insightful for the organizational co-founders in visualizing exactly how the team's cohesion and collaboration was faltering.

By contrast, another powerful moment occurred during the fourth and final working session, in which I introduced the sonic meditation exercise. During his activity, the group members were able to overcome their initial sense of self-consciousness and synchronize with each other non-verbally, through the practice of listening and improvising together, to find resonance and cohesion (Rothouse, 2018). Together, these findings from illustrate how mindfulness and contemplative arts practices can both reveal a lack of cohesion among teams and workgroups, and help to facilitate a deeper sense of resonance and meaningful collaboration.

These examples reveal how team identity matters and relates to all of the elements of group creativity and collaboration discussed so far. With this in mind, organizational efforts to support team cohesion and collaboration should examine how each individual is relating to the larger collective and to their role within it. In order to be effective, teams must feel a clear and collective sense of purpose. At the same time, is also important to recognize in the context of such efforts how some degree of initial chaos and confusion, or tension and uncertainty, can actually lead to insight, by illuminating where teams are stuck and how they may find a way forward.

Mindfulness and Contemplative Arts Exercises for Team Cohesion and Collaboration

The exercises presented in this section are intended to help develop team cohesion and collaboration through mindfulness and contemplative arts activities as well as basic principles of theatrical and sound improvisation. The specific skills addressed here build upon those discussed in the previous chapter on trust and communication, emphasizing listening, nonjudgmental awareness, attunement, and mindfulness of the wider system in which one is operating. These exercises can also help to reveal the ways in which teams have yet to fully coalesce, or where their collaboration is faltering, which can be extremely useful information for team leaders to further develop their teams' cohesion and collaboration.

Group Gesture Exercise

Context/Purpose

This simple exercise, inspired by my experiences with theatrical improvisation, is very useful both as an icebreaker for groups who are just beginning to collaborate as well as for established teams. It helps people get out of their heads and into their bodies and requires that each person attend to and attune with the other members of the group. It also introduces a sense of playfulness and fun into the group dynamic. This exercise is a great introduction to principles of improvisation and works well as a warm-up to the following exercises or to other kinds of improvisational activities.

Practice Instructions, Part 1

Ask participants to stand in a circle. Explain that this is an improv exercise in which each person will make a unique gesture, which the others will mimic. The facilitator will start by making a gesture (this can be a small hand gesture or a full-body posture), and then the full group responds by mimicking the gesture. Continue on around the circle, with each group member making a unique gesture and the group mimicking it until everyone in the group has had a turn.

Practice Instructions, Part 2

Once each person in the circle has made a gesture and it is once again the facilitator's turn, explain that now each person will make their same unique gesture, but that this time the person making the gesture will "toss" their gesture to the person standing next to them (continuing around the circle in the same direction as before). The receiver will "catch" the other person's gesture by mimicking it and will then do their own gesture and "toss" it to the next person. Continue around the circle again until each person has received and tossed a gesture.

Practice Instructions, Part 3
Once everyone has had a turn going around the circle in order, the level of difficulty increases. The facilitator can now "toss" their gesture to anyone else in the circle, first making eye contact with that person so the receiver knows to receive the gesture. Once again, the receiver "catches" the gesture by mimicking it, and then can "toss" their own gesture to anyone else in the circle. This round requires a greater degree of awareness, attention, and attunement because no one knows in advance who will receive the thrower's gesture, so everyone must pay close attention to who is throwing the gesture in any given moment and be willing to make eye contact with that person as well as with the person they will be throwing the gesture to next. Allow this round to continue until everyone has had several turns receiving and tossing gestures. If desired, the facilitator can increase the level of difficulty even more by increasing the speed of the exchange.

Debrief and Discussion
Ask participants about their experience of this exercise, including what they noticed in each round of play. Often people will describe feeling awkward or self-conscious at first, but once they become more engaged in the game, particularly during Round 3, they don't have time to think and must simply be present to the exercise. Ask what skills were needed for the exercise, and how this changed in each round. Invite them to think about and discuss how this exercise might relate to their team dynamics, including how they might incorporate the skills they practiced during this exercise in their team collaborations.

Group Movement and Creation Exercise

Context/Purpose

Building on the principles of movement and improvisation introduced in the previous exercise, this activity truly embodies the process of group creative collaboration, as each participant has the opportunity to both offer a gesture or posture to the group, and also to join with and build upon what the others already offered. This exercise incorporates the Improv principle of "yes, and…" which means saying yes to whatever others have offered and building upon it rather than rejecting or refuting what has occurred in the process of improvisation up to that point (Leonard & Yorton, 2015). This exercise is inspired by similar games from theatrical improvisation, such as the group exercise of building a machine, though this exercise is more tailored to the team context.

Practice Instructions, Part 1

In this exercise, the group engages with the process of collaboration by creating something together using a series of physical gestures or postures, with each person in turn adding to what has already been created. It is useful to begin with the previous group gesture exercise as a warm-up activity and to familiarize the group with this kind of improv game. First, ask participants to again stand in a circle, and invite each person in turn to create a movement, along with a sound effect that embodies their best self at work, in their particular role. Invite the group to witness each person's movement, going in sequence around the circle until each person has had a turn.

Practice Instructions, Part 2

Once each person has shared their sound and movement, and been witnessed by the group, ask one person to step into the middle of the circle and to again share their sound and movement. Then ask another person to step into the middle and add their sound and movement in a meaningful way to what the first person is already doing so that the two are in some kind of dialogue or interaction. Then ask another person to add their sound and movement into the mix so that all three are moving and making sound together. Continue on in this way until every team member is participating. The exercise can also be repeated by changing the order and starting with a different team member going into the circle first with others following in a different order. Notice how this changes the interaction.

The facilitator should closely observe what is created, as well as how each person is contributing to the larger whole. Pay particular attention to how the team is working together, including how closely people are standing to each other, whether they are in physical contact or separated, to what degree they are interacting with one another, and how well they seem to be working together. The facilitator can then share this feedback during the debrief to see what further insights may emerge from it about the underlying team dynamics.

Practice Instruction, Part 3

This portion of the exercise can be used for active brainstorming and creative ideation related to a particular creative task or challenge the team is currently working on. In this round, one person begins with a movement related to the creative challenge, and then each team member in turn adds a new movement that builds upon what is already happening in the circle until each person is participating. This improvisational exercise may actually lead to new insight about how to address the creative problem in question. This process can also be done multiple times, with different people starting the process. This version of the activity physically embodies the creative and iterative processes underlying design thinking and lean innovation.

Debrief and Discussion

First, ask the group about their experiences of this exercise in a general sense, including simply what they noticed or observed during the exercise. After they have shared their initial impressions, ask some more specific follow-up questions, such as:

- What were the differences between Round 2, in which each person came into the circle with an existing movement versus Round 3, in which each person added a fresh movement based on what was already happening in the circle?
- What "worked" and what didn't work with respect to the team's cohesion and collaboration in the context of this exercise?
- Did the process mirror any pre-existing dynamics of interaction or collaboration among the team members?
- Did any insights emerge with respect to the group's creative process and team interaction?
- How might these observations and insights relate to the team's day-to-day functioning and to specific creative problems the group is working on?

As I described earlier in this chapter, when I led a variation of this exercise with the group from my doctoral research study, it clearly illuminated how the group was not functioning as a cohesive team. In that instance, one of the co-founders noted that some people seemed to feel more comfortable joining their gestures with their colleagues, while others held back, preferring not to make physical contact. This led to an insight that the team was not yet comfortable operating as a cohesive unit. Although the organizational co-founders had labeled the group a "team," the reality was more of a loosely affiliated work group. Once this became clear, it had a meaningful impact on the process of organizational change we were experiencing, and the new membership model that resulted from this change. This helped the leaders understand the limitations for group creativity and collaboration among that particular group of individuals in its then-current configuration, and allowed them to set more reasonable expectations for the collective.

Sound Improvisation Exercise

Context/Purpose

The purpose of this exercise is to cultivate a deep level of listening and attunement to the dynamics of a given group. It is intended to help cultivate self-awareness of how one is contributing to the group's collaboration as well as a sense of connection, resonance, and interdependence with other group members and with the process of co-creation. As described above, this exercise was developed by composer Pauline Oliveros (1974) with the intention of practicing deep listening, non-judgmental awareness, and group improvisation. During the course of this activity, participants improvise together using only the sounds they can produce with their bodies and breath to create a collaborative, spontaneous soundscape.

Practice Instructions

As laid out by Oliveros (1974), there are two basic principles for this exercise: (1) always be a listener, and (2) there are no wrong notes. Share these guidelines with the participants, and ask them to arrange themselves in a circle, seated in chairs or on the floor. Invite them to close their eyes; it is important for this exercise to be done with eyes closed for two reasons. First, this is not a performance, and closing the eyes removes the element of people watching each other, which helps to reduce self-consciousness. Second, removing the visual sense allows people to tune more deeply into their auditory sense and listening faculties.

Begin with a few moments of guided or silent mindfulness meditation practice, attending to the breath. After a few minutes of mindful breathing together, invite participants to begin making the outbreath more and more audible, adding in the element of sound. Continue making sound on the outbreath for a few moments, inviting the group to experiment with making different sounds. The facilitator can lead with an example by making different kinds of sounds, such as using the vocal chords to create different pitches.

After a few minutes, invite the group to begin experimenting making sounds with other parts of their bodies, such as snapping, clapping, and tapping on the floor. Remind them of the two basic principles: There are no wrong notes (so there's no way to do it wrong) and always be a listener. Invite them to pause periodically, simply listening without making sound for a few moments, observing the sounds are currently happening in the circle, and then to contribute a sound that adds to, harmonizes with, or contrasts with what is already happening. Allow this process to continue organically without further instruction for several more minutes, allowing the sound to dissipate on its own or bringing the exercise to a conclusion by inviting the group to return to silent, mindful breathing. The exercise can last as long as the energy of the group continues, or as time allows; five to ten minutes is a good starting point.

Debrief and Discussion

Once again, ask participants about their overall experience of this exercise, including what they noticed about their own process and approach as well as what they observed about the group process. More specific questions could include:

- Were there any notable moments, including particular sounds, rhythms, or patterns that emerged?
- Did they perceive moments of harmony or discord?
- Were people really listening to one another or simply doing their own thing?
- What kinds of non-verbal and non-visual communication did they observe taking place?
- Did the improvisation take on a particular tone, shape, or arc?
- What was it like to return to silence after making sound together? (Often people become more aware of ambient sounds, and even the symphony of sound, that is always happening around us)

- How might this exercise inform the group's day-to-day collaborative process? What might it look and feel like to incorporate the principles of deep listening and non-judgmental awareness to their team's creative process?

In my doctoral research, when debriefing this exercise, the co-researchers expressed feeling both an initial sense of self-consciousness and a sense of playfulness in connection with the activity. Several noted how the process began with each person acting independently and that as the exercise went on, the more the group coalesced into a unified rhythm. As I described earlier in the chapter, this exercise actually helped to shift the group's sense of cohesion and connection, with the ensuing conversations being more open and authentic, leading to tangible organizational change.

Summary

The research and exercises described in this chapter focused on important elements of team cohesion and collaboration, including cooperation, interdependence, clarity of purpose, and goals, illustrating how mindfulness and arts-based activities such as theatrical and sound improvisation can support team cohesion and collaboration as well as reveal where cohesion and cooperation are lacking. To that end, the exercises described in the second part of the chapter focused on further developing the skills of listening, attunement, systems awareness, improvisation, and active collaboration among workgroups and teams. The following chapter, Chap. 7, continues to build upon the research and exercises described thus far, focusing on supporting creative ideation and insights among organizational teams.

References

Adler, J. (1999). *Authentic movement.* New York, NY: Jessica Kingsley.

Adler, J. (2002). *Offering from the conscious body; The discipline of authentic movement.* Rochester, VT: Inner Traditions.

Boucher, R. H. (2014). *Creative breakthrough emergence: A conversational accomplishment* (Doctoral dissertation). Retrieved from ProQuest Dissertations and Theses (UMI No: 3642065).

Byrne, E. K. (2017). *Mindful creativity: An exploration of a mindfulness intervention on workgroup creativity* (Doctoral dissertation). Retrieved from ProQuest Dissertations and Theses (UMI No: 10271540).

Chodorow, N. (1991). *Dance therapy and depth psychology: The moving imagination*. New York, NY: Brunner-Routledge.

Cleirigh, D. O., & Greaney, J. (2014). Mindfulness and group performance: An exploratory investigation into the effects of brief mindfulness intervention on group task performance. *Mindfulness, 6*, 601–609.

Duhigg, C. (2016, February 25). What Google learned from its quest to build a perfect team. *The New York Times Magazine*. Retrieved from www.nytimes.com/2016/02/28/magazine/what-google-learned-from-its-quest-to-build-the-perfect-team.html

Galbraith, A., Subrin, R., & Ross, D. (2008). Alzheimer's disease: Art, creativity, and the brain. In N. Hass-Cohen & R. Carr (Eds.), *Art therapy and clinical neuroscience* (pp. 254–269). Philadelphia, PA: Jessica Kingsley Publishers.

Giles, H., Denes, A., Hamilton, D. L., & Hajda, J. M. (2009). Striking a chord: A prelude to music and intergroup relations research. *Group Processes & Intergroup Relations, 12*(3), 291–301.

Halprin, D. (1999). Living artfully: Movement as an integrative process. In S. K. Levine & E. G. Levine (Eds.). *Foundations of expressive arts therapy: Theoretical and clinical perspectives*. Philadelphia, PA: Jessica Kingsley Publishers.

Halprin, D. (2003). *The expressive body in life, art and therapy: Working with movement, metaphor and meaning*. Philadelphia, PA: Jessica Kingsley Publishers.

Hess von Ludewig, H. K. (2014). *Networked creativity: Understanding the process and effect of interpersonal and networked interactions on workplace creativity* (Doctoral dissertation). Retrieved from ProQuest Dissertations and Theses (UMI No: 3647627).

Holm, M. (2014). Cultivating alternate mindsets to restructure the global economy by reducing stress and enhancing innovation. *The Business and Management Review, 5*(1), 279–289.

Homann, K. B. (2010). Embodied concepts of neurobiology in dance/ movement therapy practice. *American Journal of Dance Therapy, 32*(2), 80–99.

John-Steiner, V. (2000). *Creative collaboration*. New York, NY: Oxford University Press.

John-Steiner, V. (2011). Collaboration. In M. Runco & S. Pritzker (Eds.), *Encyclopedia of creativity* (2nd ed., pp. 222–225). San Diego, CA: Academic Press.

Leonard, K., & Yorton, T. (2015). *Yes, And: How improvisation reverses "No, But" thinking and improves creativity and collaboration—Lessons from the Second City*. New York, NY: HarperCollins.

Levine, E. G., & Levine, S. K. (Eds.). (2011). *Art in action: Expressive arts therapy and social change*. Philadelphia, PA: Jessica Kingsley Publishers.

Marlow, S. L., Lacerenza, C. N., Woods, A. L., & Salas, E. (2018). Training creativity in teams. In R. Reiter-Palmon (Ed.), *Team creativity and innovation* (pp. 283–306). New York, NY: Oxford University Press.

O'Brien, K. (2016, December 9). Listening as activism: The "Sonic meditations" of Pauline Oliveros. *The New Yorker*. Retrieved from https://www.newyorker.com/culture/culture-desk/listening-as-activism-the-sonic-meditations-of-pauline-oliveros

Oliveros, P. (1974). *Sonic meditations*. Baltimore, MD: Smith Publications.

Osborne, W. (2000). *Sounding the abyss of otherness: Pauline Oliveros' deep listening and the sonic meditations* (originally published as Chap. 3 of *Women making art*). Retrieved from http://www.osborne-conant.org/oliveros.htm

Rogers, N. (1993). *The creative connection: Expressive arts as healing*. Palo Alto, CA: Science & Behavior Books, Inc.

Rogers, N. (2011). *The creative connection for groups: Person-centered expressive arts for healing and social change*. Palo Alto, CA: Science & Behavior Books, Inc.

Rothouse, M. (2018). *Facilitating team creativity and collaboration using mindfulness and contemplative arts* (Doctoral dissertation). Retrieved from ProQuest Dissertations and Theses (Order No. 10823776).

Rozovsky, J. (2015, November 17). The five keys to a successful Google team. Retrieved from https://rework.withgoogle.com/blog/five-keys-to-a-successful-google-team/

Sawyer, K. (2017). *Group genius: The creative power of collaboration* (2nd ed.). New York, NY: Basic Books.

Serifsoy, I. (2012). *The leader's muse: An exploration of how artistic sensibilities inform organizational leadership* (Doctoral dissertation). Retrieved from ProQuest Dissertations and Theses (Order No: 3509462).

Serlin, I. (1993). Root images of healing in dance therapy. *American Journal of Dance Therapy, 15*(2), 65–76.

Smith, T. D. (2014). *Using the expressive arts to facilitate group music improvisation and individual reflection: Expanding consciousness in music learning for self-development* (Doctoral dissertation). Retrieved from ProQuest Dissertations and Theses (Order No: 3645985).

Stromsted, T. (2009). Authentic movement: A dance with the divine. *Body, Movement and Dance in Psychotherapy Journal, 4*, 201–213.

Vera, D., & Crossan, M. (2005). Improvisation and innovative performance in teams. *Organization Science, 16*(3), 203–224. https://doi.org/10.1287/orsc.1050.0126

West, M. A. (1995). Creative values and creative visions in teams at work. In C. M. Ford & D. A. Gioia (Eds.), *Creative action in organizations: Ivory tower visions & real world voices* (pp. 71–77). Thousand Oaks, CA: Sage Publications.

Whitehouse, M. (1999). *Authentic movement*. New York, NY: Jessica Kingsley.

CHAPTER 7

Creative Ideation and Insights

Abstract The first section of this chapter discusses research and scholarship on group creative ideation, including the benefits and drawbacks of processes like group brainstorming. It then describes how and when mindfulness and contemplative arts practices can support creative ideation and insights in groups. The second section offers a series of exercises and activities that facilitators can use to support creative ideation in teams and workgroups in the context of learning and development trainings, workshops, and organizational retreats. The research and exercises presented in this chapter shift the focus from the more relational dynamics of empathy, trust, communication, cohesion, and collaboration discussed in Chaps. 5 and 6 to the actual process of idea generation and techniques related to perspective shifting and insight.

Keywords Creative ideation • Insights • Brainstorming • Mindfulness • Contemplative arts

Mindful Structures for Group Creative Ideation and Problem Solving

As I was completing the coursework for my PhD program, the university where I studied was in the midst of a major organizational change, under new leadership, and newly affiliated with an academic consortium based in

M. J. Rothouse, *A Mindful Approach to Team Creativity and Collaboration in Organizations*, Palgrave Studies in Creativity and Innovation in Organizations,
https://doi.org/10.1007/978-3-030-47675-5_7

another state. These changes had been necessary to keep the school financially viable but there were a number of changes in faculty and staff, and many feared that the school was losing the very things that made it unique, along with the particular values on which it had been founded. People were angry and confused, and it was clear that something needed to happen. Because the school's residential conferences at the beginning of each semester allowed students to submit presentations and workshops, a couple of my colleagues and I who were studying psychology, creativity, and transformative social change submitted a proposal for a group processing experience to address this moment of change and uncertainty. All university stakeholders (faculty, staff, and students) were invited.

The event was very well attended by these stakeholders, including a number of faculty members, the provost, and the university president, filling up an entire ballroom of the conference center. We arranged the chairs in large circle, at which everyone would have an equal spot. We began with a few minutes of guided meditation, followed by a structured sharing using the ancient practice of a talking stick, which was passed around the circle to each person in turn. Each participant had two to three minutes to share whatever was on their minds and in their hearts with respect to the changes happening at the university. Each individual thus had the opportunity to speak and simply be heard without crosstalk or response. This in itself was a very powerful exercise, as people shared their fears and concerns as well as their passion and care for the institution and its members.

Once everyone had spoken into the circle, we opened to the conversation up to any additional comments or thoughts, again without crosstalk or debate. We then transitioned into a brainstorming exercise people wrote down on post-it notes their ideas about the major values and priorities for the school moving forward. They were encouraged to share whatever they wanted the leadership to know regarding the next phase of the university's development. These ideas were documented and formally presented to the university leadership for consideration in navigating this time of profound organizational change.

After the event, many people thanked us for providing this opportunity to share in this way, saying it felt like the most open and authentic dialogue they had experienced in connection with the institution during this transition. While many difficult decisions still lay ahead for the university, not all of them popular, this opportunity for structured conversation and feedback represented a major milestone. One of the most tangible results of this dialogue was the formation of a much stronger and more organized student government with official channels of communication to the university president and leadership, with an official role in institutional decision-making. This story illustrates how mindfulness-based group processes can support creative ideation and insight among teams and organizations, which is the focus of this chapter.

Theory and Research on Group Creative Ideation and Insights

This chapter first discusses research and scholarship on group creative ideation, including the benefits and drawbacks of processes like group brainstorming. It then describes how and when mindfulness and contemplative arts practices can support creative ideation and insights in groups. Next, it offers a series of exercises and activities that facilitators can use to support creative ideation in teams and workgroups in the context of learning and development trainings, workshops, and organizational retreats. The research and exercises presented in this chapter shift the focus from the more relational dynamics of empathy, trust, communication, cohesion, and collaboration discussed in Chaps. 5 and 6 to the actual process of idea generation and techniques related to perspective shifting and insight.

Research into group creative ideation and brainstorming has largely refuted early claims of the overall benefits of group brainstorming efforts over individual brainstorming, with subsequent studies teasing out the social and cognitive factors influencing brainstorming in group contexts. A major challenge of group brainstorming is that the social dynamics of groups often tend toward conformity and convergence rather than toward novel ideation and divergence (Paulus, Dzindolet, & Kohn, 2012). Another hindrance to group creative ideation is the rejection of potentially innovative ideas by group members if they are initially perceived to be unrealistic or difficult to implement (Rietzschel, Nijstad, & Stroebe, 2019).

To support effective brainstorming in groups, researchers have emphasized the benefits of structured, facilitator-led brainstorming sessions that limit the group size to a small number, allow for breaks, require each individual to write down their ideas, and include some element of accountability (Paulus & Brown, 2003; Paulus & Kenworthy, 2019). As Sawyer

(2017) explained, "the key to innovation is always to manage a subtle balance of planning, structure, and improvisation" (p. 34). In addition, Nemeth and O'Connor (2019) underscored the importance of articulated dissent and disagreement within teams to avoid the pitfalls of groupthink, spark divergent thinking, and thus produce more creative ideas. Contemporary organizations embrace this approach to creativity by following principles of design thinking, rapid prototyping, and lean innovation.

Another model of collective creativity developed by Hargadon and Bechky (2006) emphasized moments where individual problem-solving efforts shift to collective processes. They described how this occurs in four particular types of group interaction, including when individuals either seek help from or give help to others in the group, as well as when they either reflectively reframe their peers' ideas or reinforce those ideas. They concluded that research on collective creativity could benefit from a greater focus on these aspects of group collaboration. Another interesting element regarding creative insights is that they don't simply happen on their own, out of nowhere; in fact, according to Sawyer (2017), such insights depend upon "previous dedication, hard work, and collaboration" (p. xv).

There are many techniques for facilitating creative ideation, insight, and change. In the world of transformational coaching for organizational leaders and teams, the process of reframing or shifting perspectives is particularly salient for new ideas and ways of being to take root. The process of perspective shifting starts with helping clients uncover the underlying assumptions and limiting beliefs driving patterns of behavior that are dysfunctional or simply limiting to their creative possibilities (Hawkins & Smith, 2014; Lee & Roberts, 2010; Oshry, 2010). Whether working with individuals or groups who are creatively blocked, it is essential to first clarify what unspoken or unacknowledged beliefs, assumptions, or agreements are at play.

Mindfulness and arts-based practices can be extremely useful for enhancing awareness both of individual and collective obstacles to creativity and collaboration, and for to helping shift perspectives, which can lead to breakthrough creative ideas as well as bigger-picture insights about group dynamics and collaborative processes. Several studies over the last decade have demonstrated how multimodal expressive arts practices and other artistic methods have been utilized in workplace settings to foster greater awareness, insight, and imagination in the workplace among leaders and teams (Car, Kanjuo-Mrcela, & Mesner-Andolsek, 2015;

Goslin-Jones, 2010, 2011; Pruetipibultham & McLean, 2010; Serifsoy, 2012; Taylor & Ladkin, 2009).

In my contemplative arts training, I learned a very powerful process for group collaboration, which resembles some of the improvisational techniques described in the previous chapter. This involves inviting a group of people to sit in a circle and then giving instructions for the structure of the collaboration, depending on the medium (calligraphy, object arranging, collaborative poetry, etc.). Once the parameters have been described and each person has access to the materials needed, one person goes into the center of the circle to create the first gesture (stroke of the ink brush, placement of an object, etc.) while the others simply observe. Then, in silence, another person goes into the circle and makes a gesture that responds to and communicates with the initial gesture while the rest of the group observes. Then another person adds a third gesture that further adds to what is already there, creating a link between the two existing gestures.

Often the exercise ends with the third gesture, and then the whole group has an opportunity to observe and discuss what has been created. Many times, the resulting work is surprising different from what the first collaborator could have imagined or created on their own. Sometimes there is an opportunity to talk about what might have been altered to produce a different effect, but often the discussion simply focuses on the creators' and observers' direct experience of the creative process and of the resulting work. Steven Saitzyk (2013) described this process in his book *Place Your Thoughts Here: Meditation for the Creative Mind*, and it, along with the other improvisational techniques I have learned over the years, inspired some of the following exercises.

In the context of my doctoral research group, the mindfulness and contemplative arts activities that we did together sparked important moments of creative ideation among the group as well as insights about the group's process of creative collaboration more broadly (I described several such moments in Chap. 6). In another case, as I will describe in more detail at the beginning of Chap. 8, a contemplative arts activity sparked an "aha!" moment that yielded a guiding metaphor which helped to shape the organization's change management process.

As we came to the conclusion of our mindfulness and contemplative arts workshop process, the co-researchers began to reflect on the relationship of these activities to particular aspects of the group's creative process. Some of these insights included how, as one group member observed, "each exercise tapped into a different part of the brain and elicited new ideas" (Rothouse, 2018, p. 133) as well as how the contemplative arts activities helped to shift the energy in the room when the group process began to feel stuck or stale.

Mindfulness and Contemplative Arts Exercises for Team Creative Ideation and Insight

The mindfulness and contemplative arts exercises presented in this section aim to support creative ideation and insight in dyads and groups. An important mindfulness component of these exercises is for participants to engage in a thoughtful, intentional manner, maintaining silence except as instructed, without chatter or crosstalk. The practice here is to cultivate the skills of deep listening, witnessing, and observation, with opportunities for structured feedback and sharing only at the end of each exercise.

Shifting Perspectives Exercise

Context/Purpose
This exercise can help teams explore different perspectives, which, as discussed above, is an important skill in coaching that opens up new possibilities and new ways of looking at creative challenges. It builds upon the Guided Mindfulness Meditation and Mindful Seeing exercises presented in Chap. 4, so one should to lead the group through a brief guided meditation and practice of mindful seeing before leading this exercise. This activity stimulates active noticing and observation skills, as well as divergent and associative thinking by asking people to draw connections between seemingly unrelated or irrelevant things, and thus to look at familiar problems through a different lens or perspective. It can be useful for beginning regular team meetings in a fresh way or for initiating brainstorming sessions.

Practice Instructions
Once the group has completed the exercise of mindful seeing (from Chap. 4) and has taken at least one (or possibly more) photos, ask each person to

share their images with only a brief explanation of what they saw. The explanations should focus on what was vivid or noteworthy to them about the image, or what initially caught their attention. If possible, download the images to a computer where they can be shared on a large screen or projector. Otherwise people could simply share their images using their camera phones or by uploading the images from their phones to a collaboration app or social media site. If it is not possible to share photos, simply ask each person to describe in words what they saw or noticed, and what struck them about it.

Once each person has shared their image(s) visually or shared verbally what they saw, ask the other team members to reflect on how these images and perceptions might relate to the particular creative challenge the group is working on. Perhaps there is no immediate or tangible connection, which is perfectly fine since this exercise utilizes divergent and associative thinking; in many cases the more disparate the connections, the better it is for seeing things from a different perspective or forging new and creative connections. Moving from one photo to the next, ask how each image might speak to, or offer a new perspective on, a particular challenge or problem the team is addressing or trying to solve at work. Ask each person to write down their ideas for future reference.

Debrief and Discussion

Ask what this experience was like for the group and invite people to share any insights they derived from it with respect to particular creative challenges they are working on and/or the team's overall creative process. Ask how they could incorporate this kind of practice into their ongoing creative ideation and brainstorming efforts.

Active Listening and Coaching Exercise

Context/Purpose

Building on the practices of mindful speaking and listening presented in Chap. 5, this exercise again invites participants to work in pairs, such that each partner has the opportunity both to speak and to listen. This exercise emphasizes active, empathic listening, along with the coaching skills of reflecting and asking powerful questions.

Practice Instructions: Part 1

The practice instructions for this exercise closely mirror those of the Mindful Speaking and Listening Exercise detailed in Chap. 5. Beginning with a few minutes of guided mindfulness practice, or simply taking a few breaths in silence, ask participants to get into pairs for a practice of active listening and coaching in structured dyads. The facilitator should time the exercise, giving each speaker three to five minutes to speak. Ask each pair to designate who will speak and who will listen first. The facilitator should start the timer and ring a gong or chime to begin and end the exercise.

Ask each speaker to describe a current creative problem or challenge the team is working on, focusing on carefully defining the problem or challenge (how they are framing the problem), the parameters of the problem, and how they are currently trying to solve it. During this time, the speaker has the floor and the listener should only listen with their full presence, without reacting, responding, interjecting, or crosstalk. If the speaker runs out of things to say, the pair should simply sit in silence without further discussion or dialogue until the facilitator concludes this portion of the exercise.

Next, the listener will have the opportunity to reflect back to the speaker what they heard regarding the description of the problem, the parameters of the problem, and how the team is currently working to address it. Once the listener has finished summarizing the speaker's words, they now have the opportunity to ask one or two powerful questions in order to potentially shift the speaker's perspective on the creative challenge or spark some new insight. Powerful questions are open-ended and designed to support the speaker's own creative thinking; this is not about making suggestions, offering critique or giving advice. Some powerful questions include:

- What's possible here?
- What is the opportunity?
- What does your intuition say?
- What's missing?
- What haven't you tried yet?
- What tools or resources do you need in order to solve this problem?
- How will you know when you have found the right solution?

Allow another three to five minutes for this portion of the exercise.

Once the initial listener has had the chance to reflect back what they heard from the speaker and offer a couple of powerful questions, speaker may briefly respond to the questions. Then invite each pair to return to mindful breathing in silence for a few moments. Then, invite each pair to switch roles, so that the speaker becomes the listener and vice versa. Repeat the instructions above, and ring a gong or chime to signal the end of the exercise. Again invite the pairs to return to mindful breathing, taking a few moments to observe what this experience was like for them, including the speaking and listening portions as well as the coaching elements of reflecting back and asking powerful questions.

Debrief and Discussion

Ask participants to share what it was like for them to play each role, including what they noticed in their physical bodies, emotions, and thoughts during the exercise.

- As the speaker, what was it like to be heard and witnessed in this way, and what was it like to have your words reflected back to you by the listener? What was it like to receive and respond to the powerful questions?
- As the listener/coach, what was it like to first listen without responding, and then to reflect back the speaker's words to them? What was it like to ask powerful questions without giving advice or suggestions?
- What might it be like to both listen to and be heard by your colleagues in this way in the context of your day-to-day work or organizational role?
- How might you incorporate these skills of mindful speaking, listening, reflecting, and coaching into their everyday work lives and team collaboration sessions?

Creative Ideation/Mindful Brainstorming Exercise

Context/Purpose

The purpose of this exercise is to apply the principles of mindfulness, improvisation, and contemplative arts practice to structured brainstorming. This exercise resembles more conventional mind-mapping and whiteboard-based brainstorming exercises, but with a mindful twist. The facilitator guides the process, and each team member has an equal voice and opportunity to participate. This exercise should be practiced in silence, keeping all discussion, harvesting of ideas, and debriefing for the end.

Practice Instructions

Ask each team member to write down on a piece of paper a description of the problem or creative challenge the group is trying to solve. Once each person has written down their description of the problem, ask them to go up one by one to the board and write out their description or framing of the problem. Once each person has added their description, ask the group to silently read all of the descriptions, paying particular attention to any differences in how team members are framing the problem.

Then, continuing in silence, keeping the full list of problem descriptions visible, ask one person to go to the board and draw a very simple visual sketch of what they consider to be the central element of the problem. Then ask another team member to go to the board and add another crucial element of the problem, again without discussion or dialogue, and continue until each person has had at least one turn or until everyone agrees that the problem has been fully framed in the visual format.

Next, ask one team member to go to the board and begin mapping a potential solution to the problem, starting with the most basic pathway toward it. Then ask another person to go up and add another element or potential pathway toward a solution, continuing again until each person has had at least one turn and continuing until there are no more ideas to share. Once all ideas have been added to the board, again ask the team to silently reflect on the verbal descriptions of the problem, the visual sketches of the problem, and the potential solutions to the problem, paying attention to areas of both convergence and divergence. Ask each person to write some notes about what they notice and observe about what's been mapped out, as well as what's missing (if anything) and what new possibilities may have emerged from this process.

Debrief and Discussion

In this exercise, the debrief is the opportunity to (mindfully) enter into a dialogue both about the process itself as well as any salient observations or insights about the content generated during the exercise. First, ask the group about their experience of the exercise and what it was like to participate in this silent, mindful brainstorming process. Ask how it may have been different from other kinds of brainstorming and creative ideation activities the team has done before. Then, ask what people noticed about areas of convergence and divergence in framing the problem, both in words and in drawings, as well as in the possible solutions. This is also an opportunity for team members to ask any clarifying questions about the drawings, in case anything was unclear.

Then, with respect to the content of the brainstorming itself, ask the group to discuss the following questions:

- What's missing here?
- What's necessary or unnecessary?
- How could either the framing of the problem or the potential solutions be reconfigured or reordered?
- What information are we currently lacking to solve the problem?
- How could we draw or illustrate all of this in a different way?
- Is anyone seeing the problem in a new way now?
- Is anyone seeing a path forward that they hadn't seen before?
- What insights are emerging here? How can we harvest them and incorporate them into our process?

Summary

The research and exercises described in this chapter shifted from a focus on the interpersonal elements of team creativity and collaboration discussed in the previous chapters to a focus on the process of creative collaboration itself, in the form of creative ideation and insights. The research surveyed here described the benefits and drawbacks of group brainstorming, current understandings of collective creativity, the value of perspective shifting, and how mindfulness and contemplative arts practices can support these pathways to creative ideation and insight. To that end, the exercises in this chapter aimed to develop skills in shifting perspectives and divergent thinking; mindfulness, and coaching skills of listening, reflecting, and asking powerful questions; and a mindfulness and arts-based approach to group brainstorming. The next chapter, Chap. 8, builds upon the research and exercises presented so far, and reviews current scholarship on mindful leadership to examine how leaders can foster cultures of innovation using group process techniques grounded in mindfulness.

References

Car, M., Kanjuo-Mrcela, A., & Mesner-Andolsek, D. (2015). Artful making: Use of principles of artistic creation in management. *Teorija in Praksa, 52*(3), 511–537.

Goslin-Jones, T. (2010). *The perceived effects of person-centered expressive arts on one's work experience* (Doctoral dissertation). Retrieved from ProQuest Dissertations and Theses (UMI No: 3418296).

Goslin-Jones, T. (2011). Using expressive arts to transform the workplace. In N. Rogers (Ed.), *The creative connection for groups: Person-centered expressive arts for healing and social change* (pp. 354–357). Palo Alto, CA: Science and Behavior Books.

Hargadon, A. B., & Bechky, B. A. (2006). When collections of creatives become creative collectives: A field study of problem solving at work. *Organization Science, 17*(4), 484–500.

Hawkins, P., & Smith, N. (2014). Transformational coaching. In E. Cox, T. Bachkirova, & D. A. Clutterbuck (Eds.), *The complete handbook of coaching* (pp. 228–243). Thousand Oaks, CA: Sage.

Lee, G., & Roberts, I. (2010). Coaching for authentic leadership. In J. Passmore (Ed.), *Leadership coaching: Working with leaders to develop elite performance* (pp. 17–34). London, UK: Kogan Page.

Nemeth, C. J., & O'Connor, A. (2019). Better than individuals?: Dissent and group creativity. In P. B. Paulus & B. A. Nijstad (Eds.), *The Oxford handbook of group creativity and innovation* (pp. 73–83). Oxford, UK: Oxford University Press.

Oshry, B. (2010). Coaching from a systems perspective. In J. Passmore (Ed.), *Leadership coaching: Working with leaders to develop elite performance* (pp. 187–209). London, UK: Kogan Page.

Paulus, P. B., & Brown, V. R. (2003). Enhancing ideational creativity in groups: Lessons from research on brainstorming. In P. B. Paulus & B. A. Nijstad (Eds.), *Group creativity: Innovation through collaboration* (pp. 110–136). New York, NY: Oxford University Press.

Paulus, P. B., Dzindolet, M., & Kohn, N. W. (2012). Collaborative creativity—Group creativity and team innovation. In M. Mumford (Ed.), *Handbook of organizational creativity* (pp. 327–357). London, UK: Academic Press.

Paulus, P. B., & Kenworthy, J. B. (2019). Effective brainstorming. In P. B. Paulus & B. A. Nijstad (Eds.), *The Oxford handbook of group creativity and innovation* (pp. 287–306). Oxford, UK: Oxford University Press.

Pruetipibultham, O., & McLean, G. N. (2010). The role of arts in organizational settings. *Human Resource Development Review, 9*(1), 3–25.

Rietzschel, E. F., Nijstad, B. A., & Stroebe, W. (2019). Why great ideas are often overlooked: A review and theoretical analysis of research on idea selection and

evaluation. In P. B. Paulus & B. A. Nijstad (Eds.), *The Oxford handbook of group creativity and innovation* (pp. 179–196). Oxford, UK: Oxford University Press.
Rothouse, M. (2018). *Facilitating team creativity and collaboration using mindfulness and contemplative arts* (Doctoral dissertation). Retrieved from ProQuest Dissertations and Theses (Order No. 10823776).
Saitzyk, S. (2013). *Place your thoughts here: Meditation for the creative mind*. Los Angeles, CA: First Thought Press.
Sawyer, K. (2017). *Group genius: The creative power of collaboration* (2nd ed.). New York, NY: Basic Books.
Serifsoy, I. (2012). *The leader's muse: An exploration of how artistic sensibilities inform organizational leadership* (Doctoral dissertation). Retrieved from ProQuest Dissertations and Theses (Order No: 3509462).
Taylor, S. S., & Ladkin, D. (2009). Understanding arts-based methods in managerial development. *Academy of Management Learning & Education, 8*(1), 55–69.

CHAPTER 8

Mindful Leadership and Cultures of Innovation

Abstract This chapter discusses contemporary research on organizational creativity and innovation, describing how mindfulness and contemplative arts practice can help organizational leaders harness creative insights and ideation to create a culture of innovation. The second part of the chapter offers several practical exercises that organizational leaders and facilitators can use for in strategic planning and visioning, culture building, addressing conflict, and change management.

Keywords Mindful leadership • Innovation • Organizational culture • Mindfulness • Leadership

Mindfulness and Creative Visioning

One of my favorite exercises for organizational strategic planning and visioning, inspired by my contemplative and expressive arts training (and described in more detail later in this chapter) involves asking stakeholders to first contemplate what they appreciate about their organization and what's working well, and then to reflect upon the major challenges facing the organization and areas for growth. Depending on the context and setting, I may pair this contemplation with a mindful walk around the space,

M. J. Rothouse, *A Mindful Approach to Team Creativity and Collaboration in Organizations*, Palgrave Studies in Creativity and Innovation in Organizations,
https://doi.org/10.1007/978-3-030-47675-5_8

which can be a helpful physical and environmental anchor for their contemplations. After a few minutes of reflection, I invite them to make a few notes about what came up for them and then write down on index cards with colored markers their top three appreciations and their top three challenges or areas for growth, each in a single word or phrase.

Once each person has completed their index cards, I ask them to come and place them in the center of the circle, one by one, without discussion or explanation except to share the words on the index cards as they place them. Once each person has placed their three appreciation cards, I invite the group to come and observe all of the cards together, noticing any patterns or common themes that emerge. I then invite them to come and place their challenges/areas for growth around the outside edges of the appreciation cards, and then again ask them to observe any patterns or themes. Once everyone has reviewed all of the cards as initially placed, I invite them to begin rearranging the cards, grouping them according to common themes in order to see how people's perceptions are aligning and where they are diverging. Often several major patterns begin to emerge, with respect to both what is working well and areas for growth and development.

Often these patterns and themes can help to pave the way for a more formal conversation around strategic planning and help to identify specific initiatives for short- and long-range planning. Occasionally, a major insight or "aha" moment arises out of this exercise. When I led a group through this exercise as part of my dissertation research, such a moment of insight arose as they began to rearrange the index cards when one of the organizational co-founders commented that the cards were beginning to take on the shape of a tree. Following this observation, a few of the other members began to more intentionally play with the tree image, arranging cards related to the organization's core values and strengths to form the roots, people and systems that were already working well to create the trunk, and areas for growth and more aspirational goals to make up the branches.

I took the following photos after the group initially placed their appreciation cards, and then again at the end of the exercise, once they had rearranged both sets of cards into the shape of a tree (Figs. 8.1 and 8.2):

This image of the tree became a powerful symbol for the group with respect to our collective aspirations for the organization, which helped to guide subsequent conversations and became a touchstone for the culture building and change management process for the remainder of our work together.

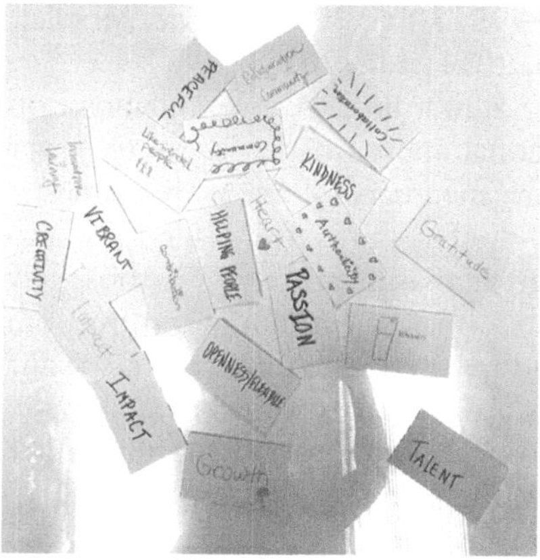

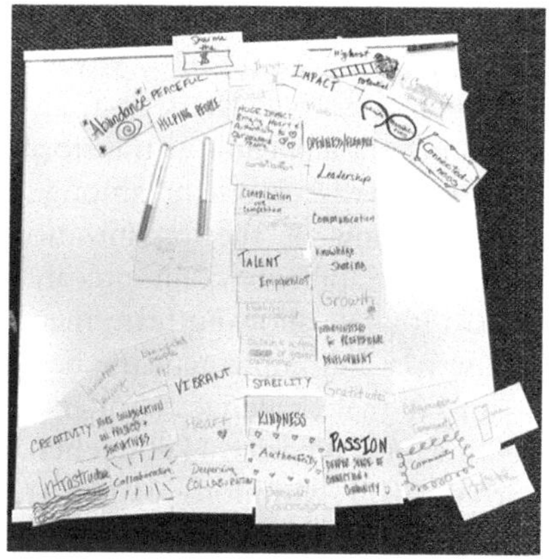

Figs. 8.1 and 8.2 Images from strategic planning and visioning exercise. (Photos by Melinda Rothouse (2018))

Theory and Research on Mindful Leadership and Creativity

This chapter discusses contemporary research on organizational creativity and innovation, describing how mindfulness and contemplative arts practice can help organizational leaders harness creative insights and ideation to create a culture of innovation. The second part of the chapter offers several practical exercises that can be useful for work with organizational leaders in strategic planning and visioning, culture building, as well as addressing conflict and change management.

The relationship between leadership and team creativity and collaboration involves a number of elements, some of which I have touched on in earlier chapters but will summarize again here specifically in the context of organizational leadership. As described in Chap. 5, the very same qualities of trust and communication that are essential for team effectiveness are also vital for leadership effectiveness in fostering organizational creativity and innovation, including mindfulness, self-awareness, emotional intelligence, and agility, as well as the kinds of listening, communication, and relational skills that allow leaders to connect with their team members in a meaningful and inspiring way, and the ability to both receive and offer honest feedback (Agars et al., 2012; Alencar, 2012; Anderson & Adams,

2016, 2019; David, 2016; Goleman, 1995/2005, 2011; Ivcevic, Moeller, Menges, & Brackett, 2020; Miyashiro, 2011; Tan, 2012).

Other essential leadership traits for stewarding creative collaboration and innovation include a transformational approach that seeks to foster growth and development among team members, along with a holistic understanding of the organizational system. Effective leadership also requires the ability to communicate a greater vision and move purposefully toward it while allowing team members sufficient autonomy and freedom to discover and implement the best and most creative solutions to specific organizational challenges (Anderson & Adams, 2016; Amabile & Khaire, 2008; Klotz, Wheeler, Halbesleben, Brock, & Buckley, 2012; Mumford & Barrett, 2011; Mumford, Mulhearn, Watts, Steele, & McIntosh, 2018).

Organizational leaders have a major role in developing, upholding, and changing the cultures of their organizations. According to a review article on leadership and organizational culture in the *Harvard Business Review*, Groysberg, Lee, Price, and Cheng (2018) emphasized the most salient elements of organizational culture as the level and quality of interpersonal interactions as well as how the organization responds to change. When leaders put their intention into cultivating positive organizational cultures, the results can be profound, as described in the recent O.C. Tanner 2020 Global Culture Study:

> When companies adopt a more connected, collaborative, and mentoring approach to leadership, they see massive improvements in the employee experience, all six essential elements of workplace culture, engagement, great work, and the likelihood to recommend the company. There's also less burnout, fewer layoffs, and increased revenue. On the other hand, organizations with traditional leadership styles see dramatic decreases in the employee experience and all areas of workplace culture, higher burnout rates, and an increased odds of layoffs. ("Leadership," 2019, para. 17–18)

The Society for Human Resource Management also detailed a recent study examining the costs of a toxic workplace culture (Mirza, 2019). This research highlights the influence that leaders have on their organizational cultures and the consequences of not attending to issues of workplace culture.

To help address questions of leadership and culture, the concept of mindful leadership suggests that mindfulness practices can help leaders to cultivate the kinds of self-awareness, communication, and relational skills necessary for both effective leadership and organizational creativity and innovation. According to Janice Marturano (2013) of the Institute for Mindful Leadership, "a mindful leader is someone who embodies leadership presence by cultivating focus, clarity, creativity and compassion in the service of others" (para. 1). Carroll (2010, 2011) characterized mindful leaders as those who see the interconnected nature of their organizations and teams, communicate their visions and intentions clearly, bring people together in service of a common vision, and approach organizational challenges with open-mindedness rather than thinking they always have the answers.

Similarly, Erlich (2015) described how principles of mindful leadership can support leaders' sense of confidence and self-acceptance while deepening their understanding of the teams they lead and focusing on the creative process as well as on specific outcomes. Several recent studies have investigated the effects of mindfulness training on leadership and the mechanisms underlying them, demonstrating that mindfulness skills are particularly useful in helping leaders to manage tasks more intentionally; to become more self-reflective; to relate, develop trust, and communicate with others in their organizations more effectively; and to adapt to change more successfully (Arendt, Pircher Verdorfer, & Kugler, 2019; Rupprecht et al., 2019; Stedham & Skaar, 2019).

A particularly useful model for helping leaders manage organizational change and transformation that is based in principles of mindfulness is the Theory U framework, developed by Massachusetts Institute of Technology (MIT) professor and organizational leadership expert Otto Scharmer (2009, 2013), which grew out of his earlier collaboration with a group of colleagues exploring the concept of *presence* in managing organizational change:

> We first thought of presence as being fully conscious and aware in the present moment. Then we began to appreciate presence as deep listening, of being open beyond one's preconceptions and historical ways of making sense. We came to see the importance of letting go of old identities and the need to control and…making choices to serve the evolution of life. Ultimately, we came to see all these aspects of presence as leading to a state of "letting come," of consciously participating in a larger field for change. When this happens, the field shifts, and the forces shaping a situation can move from re-creating the past to manifesting or realizing an emerging future. (Senge, Scharmer, Jaworski, & Flowers, 2004, pp. 13–14)

The *presencing* approach requires that leaders refrain from thinking that they already know the answers and instead approach complex organizational problems from a place of curiosity, openness, and observation in order to discern the best way forward.

The Theory U model (Scharmer, 2009, 2013, 2018) incorporates the principle of presence into a five-stage process that involves (1) Co-initiating, (2) Co-sensing, (3) Co-presencing, (4) Co-creating, and (5) Co-evolving. At each stage of this collaborative process, leaders must work cooperatively with organizational stakeholders from a place of mindful receptivity in order to develop truly innovative solutions to the complex challenges that contemporary organizations currently face. Along with his colleagues at the Presencing Institute, Scharmer has helped guide a number of organizations using a more mindful approach to change management and is now sharing these insights with the broader public with his MIT U.Lab course, a massive open online course (MOOC) that is available to anyone seeking to learn the principles of presencing and Theory U.

Another useful tool for mindful leadership is the conversational or inclusive leadership model (Brown, 2002; Brown & Isaacs, 2005; Agger-Gupta & Harris, 2017), which offers a structure for dialogue in real-world organizational settings to harvest the wisdom and knowledge of all key stakeholders to foster positive change and transformation. The World Café process, a conversational leadership technique, uses creative processes and storytelling to foster knowledge creation and collaborative inquiry (Brown, 2002; Brown & Isaacs, 2005). A version of the World Café process is detailed as an exercise later in this chapter.

One of the overall benefits of the mindfulness and contemplative arts process for the organizational leaders who participated in my doctoral research study was that it helped them to identify common goals and values while also helping them to better understand their team's creative process. Another insight that emerged was the need for the leaders of the organization to articulate a clearer mission and structure to the team for achieving specific projects and organizational goals (Rothouse, 2018).

Mindfulness and Contemplative Arts Exercises for Creative Leadership and Innovation

The exercises presented in this section give leaders specific mindfulness-based and contemplative arts-inspired tools to more effectively facilitate open discussion and dialogue among their teams and stakeholders, creatively approach strategic planning and visioning sessions, and navigate conflict and change within their organizations.

Inclusive Leadership and Culture-Building Exercise

Context/Purpose

This exercise is inspired by research on inclusive, conversational leadership and the World Café process (Brown, 2002; Brown & Isaacs, 2005) for facilitating group dialogue and transformative change. The purpose of the exercise is to facilitate mindful dialogue regarding organizational culture and/or organization-wide challenges among members and stakeholders.

Practice Instructions

In this group process for addressing creative challenges and culture-building efforts, the facilitator first leads the group in a brief mindfulness exercise and then poses a question or series of questions for the group to contemplate. These questions will be developed by the facilitator in collaboration with organizational leaders. Allow all participants to reflect on the question or questions, write down their thoughts on paper, and/or draw their responses using any available pens, markers, or other drawing materials. Allow 10–15 minutes for this individual contemplation.

Then ask the participants to split into several different groups (depending on the number of people in attendance); each group should designate a note taker and a conversation host who will also act as the group's designated speaker. Ask the members of each group to share their reflections and ideas regarding the questions that were posed by the facilitator. Once each person has shared their thoughts they can engage in a period of discussion and dialogue regarding the questions posed. The note taker for each group should write down the main points and themes from the group discussion on a large post-it note. Allow another 10 minutes or so for this portion of the exercise.

Next, ask all group members except the hosts to move to different groups (people who were in the same group initially should disperse into new groups so that the group composition will be different each time). The hosts should stay in their initial spot, acting as the anchor point for each of their groups. Repeat the process with the new groups, with each group designating a new note taker. Once the second set of groups has completed the process, ask the groups to again reconfigure themselves, with existing group members dissolving into new groups and hosts remaining in their spots. Repeat the process one final time in these new group configurations, and then ask everyone to come back to the full-group circle or initial configuration of the room.

Once the full group is reassembled, ask each of the hosts to share the main points written down by each of their scribes during the three different group iterations. Once each host has shared the major discussion points of each of their three groups, the facilitator can guide a larger group discussion of the major themes that emerged and point toward any specific action steps that have arisen out of the dialogic process.

Debrief and Discussion
Invite participants to share their experiences of the exercise, including any observations about how the group process worked in their small groups and when sharing their ideas with the larger group. Ask them to reflect on how they could use this exercise in their ongoing leadership and culture-building efforts.

Strategic Planning and Visioning Exercise

Context/Purpose
As described at the beginning of this chapter, I developed this exercise as a synthesis of my training in mindfulness, contemplative arts, and expressive arts. I have found that it can be very useful in combination with more traditional strategic planning efforts, adding a more reflective and creative approach. The exercise first asks participants to reflect individually on organizational strengths and challenges, and then to write them out on index cards with colored markers, and finally to present them to the group in the center of the circle.

This visually oriented approach to creating and presenting the cards allows participants to immediately begin making connections between different peoples' ideas and perceptions. The subsequent rearrangement of the cards allows the group to quickly discern common themes and begin to prioritize them. As in the example from the beginning of the chapter, sometimes this exercise can spur important insights based on the patterns that begin to emerge, which can further inform the strategic planning and visioning process.

Practice Instructions
Ask the participants to arrange their chairs into a circle and begin with a few minutes of mindfulness meditation practice. Then explain the purpose and context for this exercise as described above. Hand out six index cards

to each participant, along with colored markers for writing. Ask the assembled group to first contemplate what they appreciate about the organization, including what's working well, and what they consider to be the organization's strengths. This may be paired with a mindful walk around the space to help support their reflections, particularly if the exercise is taking place within the actual workplace.

Ask them to jot down any ideas that come to mind and then to distill those thoughts down to their top three appreciations or strengths, each communicated in a single word or phrase, which they should write on three of the index cards with a marker in capital letters. Then ask them to repeat this process, now contemplating what they see as the major challenges or areas of growth for the organization, and then writing down their top three on their remaining index cards with a marker. Once each person has finished writing down both their appreciations/strengths and challenges/areas for growth, ask them to reassemble into a circle with plenty of space in the center.

Next, ask each person, one-by-one, to share the three words or phrases indicating their appreciations and organizational strengths written on their index cards, coming into the middle of the circle to place their cards. This should be done without conversation or crosstalk, with the full group witnessing and observing each person's placement of their cards until everyone in the group has had a turn. Then invite the participants to move closer so that they can see all of the cards together, observing any common themes or patterns that seem to be emerging. Then ask everyone to return to their seats at the outside of the circle.

Next, ask each person in turn to come and place their three cards indicating challenges/areas for growth in an outer ring beyond the appreciations/strengths, so that they form a concentric circle outside of the appreciations/strengths. Once each person has placed all three of their remaining cards, again invite the group to come closer to observe any themes or patterns that are emerging with respect to challenges and areas for growth. At this point, people can begin grouping duplicate or similar cards together according to the themes and patterns they are noticing. This process will quickly reveal areas of convergence and divergence in the group's perceptions of the organization's strengths and challenges.

Once the cards have been grouped together according to themes, ask if anyone is noticing a larger pattern or a different way the cards might be grouped together. As I described at the beginning of the chapter, sometimes this second round of rearranging the cards yields further insight.

Other times, the common themes simply become very clear, including the relationships between the strengths and challenges (e.g., we all value community service and we would like to find more opportunities to actually get out into the community, or we all appreciate collaboration but don't have clear avenues and structures in place in which to collaborate).

Debrief and Discussion
Ask participants about their experience of this exercise, including what they noticed about their own process and the larger group process. What struck them about this exercise? Did it help them to see themes they hadn't seen before? What about areas of divergence or disagreement? The themes, patterns, and insights generated by this exercise can lay the groundwork for more formal strategic planning and visioning efforts.

Group Process for Addressing Organizational Change or Conflict

Context/Purpose
This exercise is informed by age-old practices of sitting in circle with one's community and using a talking stick, as well as more contemporary leadership and change management processes such as presencing and Theory U (Scharmer, 2009, 2013, 2018; Senge, Scharmer, Jaworski, & Flowers, 2004). The practice of coming together in community and using a talking stick for structured sharing and conflict resolution is a common practice in many indigenous traditions (Beyer, 2016; Freeman, 2017) as well as contemporary circling and authentic relating practices (Beneteau, 2017; Gondo, 2018; The Circling™ Method, 2020) and restorative justice techniques (Van Ness & Strong, 2014). As Beyer (2016) explained:

> There are practical reasons for sitting in a circle. Everyone can see everyone else. No one is in front, and no one can hide in the back. But the circle is symbolic as well. The circle indicates the equality of all who sit together. There is no head of the table. Everyone's voice carries as much weight as the voice of everyone else. Everyone is out front, equally accountable for their words. (n.p.)

This is an age-old, egalitarian process for addressing important issues in a community setting. Using a talking stick (or another symbolic object) allows each person in the circle the opportunity to speak their thoughts and feelings into the group without dialogue or debate; whoever has the talking stick has the floor, and all others must remain silent until they receive the talking stick, signaling that it is their turn to speak. As described in the introduction to Chap. 7, this process can be helpful for organizations dealing with change and conflict. While it does not necessarily generate specific community-related decisions unto itself, it can be a useful resource for moving difficult conversations forward, illuminating possible courses of action, and most importantly for ensuring that all perspectives are shared and heard by leadership in a structured and respectful way.

Practice Instructions
The facilitator should invite all attendees to arrange themselves into a circle. The facilitator can act as timekeeper or designate a timekeeper. Explain the instructions for using the talking stick: each person has a specific amount of time (two to five minutes depending on time constraints) to speak from a place of openness and authenticity about the topic at hand without dialogue, debate, or crosstalk. People may also choose to simply pass if they have nothing to say at this time. Once the talking stick has been passed all the way around the circle and everyone has had a chance to speak, there could be an opportunity to go around again if there is more to be said, or the facilitator could open up the floor for a more free-style discussion (still passing the talking stick to whoever would like to speak so the conversation doesn't degenerate into argument or debate).

Once the group agrees that all important ideas and perspectives have been shared, people can offer specific ideas, insights, or suggestions for concrete action using post-its on a whiteboard or wall, which can later be harvested by leadership for further action. If time allows, people could then also break into smaller groups or teams to further discuss specific ideas or themes that came up in the circle and begin to create plans for meaningful action.

Debrief and Discussion
Ask participants about their experience of this exercise, including what they noticed about the group process of using the circle and talking stick. How did this process resemble or differ from their usual experiences of organizational meetings and information-sharing processes? What did they learn from the circle that they did not know before? Did any new insights or ways to view the problem or possible solutions come to light? How might they carry this conversation forward with follow-up conversations or tangible action steps? How might organizational stakeholders utilize this process to find a new way forward?

Summary

The research and exercises described in this chapter focused on mindful leadership and the role of organizational leaders in creating a culture of innovation. The research reviewed here detailed specific leadership traits, skills, and processes that support effective leadership, team creativity, positive workplace cultures, and organizational innovation. The exercises in this chapter included several group process activities for inclusive leadership and culture building, strategic planning and visioning, and addressing organizational change and conflict.

References

Agars, M. D., Kaufman, J. C., Deane, A., & Smith, B. (2012). Fostering individual creativity through organizational context: A review of recent research and recommendations for organizational leaders. In M. Mumford (Ed.), *Handbook of organizational creativity* (pp. 271–291). San Diego, CA: Academic Press.

Agger-Gupta, N., & Harris, B. (2017). Dialogic change and the practice of inclusive leadership. In A. Boitano, R. L. Dutra, & H. E. Schockman (Eds.), *Breaking the zero-sum game: Transforming societies through inclusive leadership* (pp. 305–322). Bingley, UK: Emerald Publishing Limited.

Alencar, E. M. L. S. (2012). Creativity in organizations: Facilitators and inhibitors. In M. Mumford (Ed.), *Handbook of organizational creativity* (pp. 87–111). San Diego, CA: Academic Press.

Amabile, T. M., & Khaire, M. (2008, October). Creativity and the role of the leader. *Harvard Business Review*. Retrieved from https://hbr.org/2008/10/creativity-and-the-role-of-the-leader

Anderson, R. J., & Adams, W. A. (2016). *Mastering leadership: An integrated framework for breakthrough performance and extraordinary business results*. Hoboken, NJ: John Wiley & Sons, Inc.

Anderson, R. J., & Adams, W. A. (2019). *Scaling leadership: Building organizational capability and capacity to create outcomes that matter most*. Hoboken, NJ: John Wiley & Sons, Inc.

Arendt, J., Pircher Verdorfer, A., & Kugler, K. G. (2019). Mindfulness and leadership: Communication as a behavioral correlate of leader mindfulness and its effect on follower satisfaction. *Frontiers in Psychology, 10*, 667. https://doi.org/10.3389/fpsyg.2019.00667

Beneteau, M. (2017). *Circling and authentic relating practice guide: Learn the group conversation practice that will transform all of your relationships and bring you the love, friendship and community that you want*. CreateSpace Independent Publishing Platform.

Beyer, S. V. (2016). *Talking stick: Peacemaking as a spiritual path*. New York, NY: Simon & Schuster.

Brown, J. (2002). *The world café: Living knowledge through conversations that matter* (Doctoral dissertation). Retrieved from ProQuest Dissertations and Theses (UMI No: 3041666).

Brown, J., & Isaacs, D. (2005). *The world café: Shaping our futures through conversations that matter*. San Francisco, CA: Berrett-Koehler Publishers, Inc.

Carroll, M. (2010, March). Beyond the elevator speech. *Shambhala Sun*, pp. 54–57.

Carroll, M. (2011). At work, don't be a know-it-all. In B. Boyce (Ed.), *The mindfulness revolution: Leading psychologists, scientists, artists, and meditation teachers on the power of mindfulness in daily life* (pp. 97–100). Boulder, CO: Shambhala Publications.

David, S. (2016). *Emotional agility: Get unstuck, embrace change, and thrive in work and life*. New York, NY: Avery.

Erlich, J. (2015). Creating mindful leaders and organizations. *People + Strategy, 38*(3), 22–25.

Freeman, R. (2017). *The talking stick way: An indigenous research methodology for engaging diverse global conversations* (Master's thesis). Retrieved from https://shareok.org/handle/11244/52926

Goleman, D. (1995/2005). *Emotional intelligence: Why it can matter more than IQ* (10th anniversary ed.). New York, NY: Bantam Books.

Goleman, D. (2011). *Leadership: The power of emotional intelligence*. Florence, MA: More Than Sound.

Gondo, E. (2018, September 20). *5 authentic relating techniques that dissolve tension in the workplace*. Conscious Company. Retrieved from https://consciouscompanymedia.com/workplace culture/authentic-relating-workplace/

Groysberg, B., Lee, J., Price, J., & Cheng, Y. (2018, January–February). The leader's guide to corporate culture. *Harvard Business Review*. Retrieved from https://hbr.org/2018/01/the-culture-factor

Ivcevic, Z., Moeller, J., Menges, J., & Brackett, M. (2020). Supervisor emotionally intelligent behavior and employee creativity. *Journal of Creative Behavior*. https://doi.org/10.1002/jocb.436

Klotz, A. C., Wheeler, A. R., Halbesleben, J. R. B., Brock, M. E., & Buckley, M. R. (2012). Can reward systems influence the creative individual? In M. Mumford (Ed.), *Handbook of organizational creativity* (pp. 607–631). San Diego, CA: Academic Press.

"Leadership." (2019). Retrieved December 26, 2019, from O.C. Tanner Global Culture Report website: https://www.octanner.com/global-culture-report/2020/leadership.html

Marturano, J. (2013, August 5). What is a 'mindful leader?'. [Web log post]. Retrieved from https://instituteformindfulleadership.org/mindful-leader/

Mirza, B. (2019, September 25). Toxic workplace cultures hurt workers and company profits. [Web log post]. Retrieved from https://www.shrm.org/resourcesandtools/hr-topics/employee-relations/pages/toxic-workplace-culture-report.aspx

Miyashiro, M. R. (2011). *The empathy factor: Your competitive advantage for personal, team, and business success.* Encinitas, CA: Puddle Jumper Press.

Mumford, M. D., & Barrett, J. D. (2011). Leadership. In M.A. Runco & S. R. Pritzker (Eds.), *Encyclopedia of creativity* (2nd ed.), Vol. 1 (pp. 41–46). San Diego, CA: Academic Press.

Mumford, M. D., Mulhearn, T. J., Watts, L. L., Steele, L. M., & McIntosh, T. (2018). Leader impacts on creative teams: Direction, engagement, and sales. In R. Reiter-Palmon (Ed.), *Team creativity and innovation* (pp. 131–166). New York, NY: Oxford University Press.

Rothouse, M. (2018). *Facilitating team creativity and collaboration using mindfulness and contemplative arts* (Doctoral dissertation). Retrieved from ProQuest Dissertations and Theses (Order No. 10823776).

Rupprecht, S., Falke, P., Kohls, N., Tamdjidi, C., Wittmann, M., & Kersemaekers, W. (2019). Mindful leader development: How leaders experience the effects of mindfulness training on leader capabilities. *Frontiers in Psychology, 10*, 1081. https://doi.org/10.3389/fpsyg.2019.01081

Scharmer, C. O. (2009). *Theory U: Leading from the future as it emerges.* San Francisco, CA: Berrett-Koehler Publishers, Inc.

Scharmer, C. O. (2013, July 9). Uncovering the blind spot of leadership. Retrieved from http://www.dailygood.org/story/450/uncovering-the-blind-spot-of-leadership-c-otto-scharmer/

Scharmer, O. (2018). Leading from the future: A new social technology for our times. Retrieved from https://thesystemsthinker.com/leading-from-the-future-a-new-social-technology-for-our-times/

Senge, P., Scharmer, O. C., Jaworski, J., & Flowers, B. S. (2004). *Presence: Human purpose and the field of the future.* New York, NY: Crown Business.

Stedham, Y., & Skaar, T. B. (2019). Mindfulness, trust, and leader effectiveness: A conceptual framework. *Frontiers in Psychology, 10*, 1588. https://doi.org/10.3389/fpsyg.2019.01588

Tan, C. (2012). *Search inside yourself: The unexpected path to achieving success, happiness (and world peace).* New York, NY: HarperCollins.

"The Circling™ Method." (2020). Retrieved February 29, 2020, from The Circling Institute website: https://www.circlinginstitute.com/circling/what-is-circling/

Van Ness, D. W., & Strong, K. H. (2014). *Restoring justice: An introduction to restorative justice* (5th ed.). New York, NY: Routledge.

CHAPTER 9

Conclusion

Abstract This chapter weaves together the research and practices presented in the previous chapters. It summarizes the key findings from my research into using mindfulness and contemplative arts practices to support team creativity and collaboration, which formed the basis of this book. It also discusses how coaches, consultants, facilitators, and organizational leaders can apply the research and exercises described here in real-world organizational settings and within functioning organizational teams to support creativity, collaboration, and innovation. Finally, it discusses avenues for future research.

Keywords Mindfulness • Contemplative arts • Team creativity • Collaboration • Facilitation

In the context of my coaching, consulting, and facilitation work over the years, I have had the opportunity to work with executives, emerging leaders, and individual contributors from a broad range of organizations and industries, from non-profit foundations and startups to major corporations like Indeed, Apple, and Dell. In addition to my formal doctoral research I have had the opportunity to observe and learn from my clients where they get stuck, where communication breaks down, and what

M. J. Rothouse, *A Mindful Approach to Team Creativity and Collaboration in Organizations*, Palgrave Studies in Creativity and Innovation in Organizations,
https://doi.org/10.1007/978-3-030-47675-5_9

frustrates them most about their team experiences, as well as their leadership successes, their creative breakthroughs, and their "aha!" moments. I've also had the opportunity to lead the exercises presented in this book, and many others like them, in a variety of settings and contexts.

My biggest takeaway from these experiences is that no matter where they are in their career and leadership journeys, the vast majority of my clients desire to grow and develop themselves professionally, yet often lament the lack of formal leadership training, professional development, and mentoring opportunities they are currently receiving in their organizations. When offered tools to help develop their mindfulness, self-awareness, emotional intelligence, communication, collaboration, and leadership skills, they welcome the opportunity. In my view, such skills are needed, now more than ever, to address the creative challenges faced by contemporary organizations. The world needs leaders and innovators with high levels of self- and systems awareness, interpersonal and relating skills, an understanding of the profound interconnections among all things and all beings, and an appreciation of the consequences of even the smallest actions, in order to creatively approach the political, economic, and environmental crises we all now face as global citizens and to bring the earth into balance.

Summary and Applications of This Work

This concluding chapter weaves together the research and practices presented throughout the book. It summarizes the key findings from my research into using mindfulness and contemplative arts practices to support team creativity and collaboration, which formed the basis of this work. It also discusses how coaches, consultants, facilitators, and organizational leaders can apply the research and exercises described here in real-world organizational settings and within functioning organizational teams to support creativity, collaboration, and innovation. Finally, it discusses the limitations of this research and proposes avenues for future research.

In addition to the most current research available on mindfulness, creativity, and collaboration in organizational contexts, the preceding chapters introduced a series of mindfulness and contemplative arts-based exercises and activities that coaches, consultants, facilitators, and organizational leaders can use to support team creativity and collaboration in each of these five key areas. My hope is that the book, along with the many other excellent works and avenues of emerging research into mindfulness and organizational creativity, will help to bring these practices into a wider corporate consciousness and provide practical tools that facilitators can use to support a more mindful approach to team creativity, group collaboration, and leadership.

According to my research and experience working with organizations and teams, the mindfulness and contemplative arts processes described here may be most beneficial for organizations looking to enhance team-building efforts by supporting a deeper level of interpersonal connection and trust as well as communication, cohesiveness, and collaboration. Contemplative arts practice may also be used fruitfully by leaders to cultivate a more mindful approach to their work, as well as for visioning and strategic planning efforts, to foster and develop a more positive and open workplace culture.

The previous chapters introduced important concepts and research relevant to mindfulness and creativity in organizations, specifically focusing on how mindfulness and contemplative arts practices can help support team creativity and collaboration in five key areas, based on a model I developed from my doctoral research and professional experience with creativity, mindfulness, and leadership. These five areas include:

1. Individual-Level Mindfulness: Relaxation, Openness, and Self-Awareness
2. Trust and Authentic Communication
3. Team Cohesion and Collaboration
4. Creative Ideation and Insights
5. Leadership for Creating a Culture of Innovation

As I described in the Introduction, these five areas build upon each other, starting with individual-level mindfulness (Fig. 1.5).

This model provides a useful framework for understanding how to intentionally develop mindfulness, trust and rapport, creative collaboration, and cultures of innovation. It is a useful framework for scholars, organizational leaders, coaches, consultants, and facilitators to use in conjunction with other mindfulness and arts practices and team-building efforts.

Starting with the basic mindfulness practices described in Chap. 4 as a foundation to help foster individual-level relaxation, openness, and self-awareness, facilitators can then introduce the exercises in Chap. 5 to begin developing a deeper level of empathy, trust, and authentic communication within a particular group or team. Once a sense of openness and trust has been established, one can begin focusing on the exercises in Chap. 6 to foster group cohesion and collaboration, which can then lead naturally into creative ideation and insight, as described in the research and exercises presented in Chap. 7. Ultimately, it is the responsibility of team and organizational leaders to cultivate the leadership skills described in Chap. 8; leaders and facilitators can use the exercises presented in that chapter to further support strategic planning and visioning, culture-building efforts, and change/conflict management.

Benefits and Challenges of Mindfulness and Contemplative Arts Practices in Organizations

Some of the benefits of using mindfulness and contemplative arts practices in organizations include allowing individuals and teams to slow down, become more present to themselves and others, and develop more awareness of their own internal processes. These practices also support greater awareness of how individuals are showing up for their teams, and of the wider systems and contexts in which they are operating. Another benefit is the opportunity for individuals and teams to work through discomfort and embrace vulnerability in order to get to a place of deeper level of insight, growth, and authenticity (Brown, 2018; Goslin-Jones, 2010, 2011; Rothouse, 2018).

Another crucial element for this work is the skill and presence of the facilitator. When presented clearly, with sufficient instruction, context, and opportunity for debrief and discussion, these exercises can be transformative. A good deal of research has emphasized the importance of a mindful, compassionate presence on the part of a therapist or facilitator for doing deep work (Hanson, 2015; Rogers, 1961; Siegel, 2007, 2010; Senge, Scharmer, Jaworski, & Flowers, 2004; Scharmer, 2009), and this also holds true for facilitators working in organizations.

Of course the opposite is also true; poor facilitation can turn great content into disappointing experiences that become counterproductive to the participants, leaving them wondering why they took time out of their busy work lives to participate in a workshop or training that falls flat or feels like a waste of time. Thus it is extremely important for facilitators to cultivate their own mindfulness and facilitation skills, to learn who their clients are and to quickly glean which activities are appropriate for the particular groups they are working with. Facilitators should check in with participants regularly to see how the exercises are landing, in order to deliver their full benefits and to pivot when necessary.

A great example of this took place on the first day of a six-month leadership development program I helped to facilitate at a major technology company. After completing group introductions, the facilitators launched into an overview of the program but quickly noticed there was some sort of disconnect happening in the room. They stopped to check in about what people were experiencing, only to discover that many of the participants had just found out (some of them literally that morning) they had been chosen by their supervisors to join the program, and had no idea why. They were concerned they were in "trouble" or that this was a consequence of poor performance, when in fact the opposite was true; they had been chosen because of their leadership promise and potential. Once this conversation had taken place, the group began to open up and connect much more genuinely, and they were ready to receive and engage with the content of the program.

Opportunities for Future Research

The research and practices presented here invite possibilities for further research, both of a qualitative and quantitative nature, into the effects of mindfulness and contemplative arts practices on team creativity and collaboration in a variety of real-world organizational settings, ranging from small entrepreneurial teams, startups, and non-profits to large corporations. Such investigations could explore the effects of such practices on team creativity and collaboration over different time frames, in different organizational contexts and structures, and among different demographics. Future research could also incorporate mixed-methods designs, with specific pre-and post-intervention assessments related to mindfulness, individual and group creativity, collaboration, team cohesion, and leadership effectiveness.

References

Brown, B. (2018). *Dare to lead: Brave work, tough conversations, whole hearts.* London, UK: Vermillion.

Goslin-Jones, T. (2010). *The perceived effects of person-centered expressive arts on one's work experience* (Doctoral dissertation). Retrieved from ProQuest Dissertations and Theses (UMI No: 3418296).

Goslin-Jones, T. (2011). Using expressive arts to transform the workplace. In N. Rogers (Ed.), *The creative connection for groups: Person-centered expressive arts for healing and social change* (pp. 354–357). Palo Alto, CA: Science and Behavior Books.

Hanson, R. (2015, March 16). *What is mindful presence?* Retrieved from https://www.rickhanson.net/mindful-presence-2/

Rogers, C. (1961). *On becoming a person: A therapist's view of psychotherapy.* New York, NY: Houghton Mifflin Company.

Rothouse, M. (2018). *Facilitating team creativity and collaboration using mindfulness and contemplative arts* (Doctoral dissertation). Retrieved from ProQuest Dissertations and Theses (Order No. 10823776).

Scharmer, C. O. (2009). *Theory U: Leading from the future as it emerges.* San Francisco, CA: Berrett-Koehler Publishers, Inc.

Senge, P., Scharmer, O. C., Jaworski, J., & Flowers, B. S. (2004). *Presence: Human purpose and the field of the future.* New York, NY: Crown Business.

Siegel, D. (2007). *The mindful brain: Reflection and attunement in the cultivation of well-being.* New York, NY: W. W. Norton & Co.

Siegel, D. (2010). *The mindful therapist: A clinician's guide to mindsight and neural integration.* New York, NY: W. W. Norton & Co.

References

Agger-Gupta, N., & Harris, B. (2017). Dialogic change and the practice of inclusive leadership. In A. Boitano, R. L. Dutra, & H. E. Schockman (Eds.), *Breaking the zero-sum game: Transforming societies through inclusive leadership* (pp. 305–322). Bingley, UK: Emerald Publishing Limited.

Agnoli, S., Vanucci, M., Pelagatti, C., & Corazza, G. E. (2018). Exploring the link between mind wandering, mindfulness, and creativity: A multidimensional approach. *Creativity Research Journal, 30*(1), 41–53. https://doi.org/10.1080/10400419.2018.1411423

Alencar, E. M. L. S. (2012). Creativity in organizations: Facilitators and inhibitors. In M. Mumford (Ed.), *Handbook of organizational creativity* (pp. 87–111). San Diego, CA: Academic Press.

Amabile, T. M. (1996). *Creativity in context.* Boulder, CO: Westview Press.

Amabile, T. M. (1998). A model for creativity and innovation in organizations. *Research in Organizational Behavior, 10*, 123–167.

Amabile, T. M., & Khaire, M. (2008, October). Creativity and the role of the leader. *Harvard Business Review.* Retrieved from https://hbr.org/2008/10/creativity-and-the-role-of-the-leader

Analayo, B. (2003). *Satipatthana: The direct path to realization.* Cambridge, UK: Windhorse Publications.

Anderson, R. J., & Adams, W. A. (2016). *Mastering leadership: An integrated framework for breakthrough performance and extraordinary business results.* Hoboken, NJ: John Wiley & Sons, Inc.

M. J. Rothouse, *A Mindful Approach to Team Creativity and Collaboration in Organizations*, Palgrave Studies in Creativity and Innovation in Organizations,
https://doi.org/10.1007/978-3-030-47675-5

Anderson, R. J., & Adams, W. A. (2019). *Scaling leadership: Building organizational capability and capacity to create outcomes that matter most.* Hoboken, NJ: John Wiley & Sons, Inc.

Arendt, J., Pircher Verdorfer, A., & Kugler, K. G. (2019). Mindfulness and leadership: Communication as a behavioral correlate of leader mindfulness and its effect on follower satisfaction. *Frontiers in Psychology, 10*, 667. https://doi.org/10.3389/fpsyg.2019.00667

Auernhammer, J., & Hall, H. (2014). Organizational culture in knowledge creation, creativity and innovation: Towards the Freiraum model. *Journal of Information Science, 40*(2), 154–166.

Avalon, A. (2006). *Arts in new directions: The development and application of a construct that uses the arts to promote transformation and self-actualization in health care and education/therapy* (Doctoral dissertation). Retrieved from ProQuest Dissertations and Theses (UMI No: 3240360).

Baas, M., Nevicka, B., & Ten Velden, F. S. (2014). Specific mindfulness skills differentially predict creative performance. *Personality and Social Psychology Bulletin, 40*(9), 1092–1106.

Barner, C. P., & Barner, R. W. (2012). Mindfulness, openness to experience, and transformational learning. In *The Oxford handbook of reciprocal adult development and learning* (2nd ed.). https://doi.org/10.1093/oxfordhb/9780199736300.013.0087

Barratt, B. B. (2010). *The emergence of somatic psychology and bodymind therapy.* New York, NY: Palgrave Macmillan.

Beneteau, M. (2017). *Circling and authentic relating practice guide: Learn the group conversation practice that will transform all of your relationships and bring you the love, friendship and community that you want.* CreateSpace Independent Publishing Platform.

Berkovich-Ohana, A., Glicksohn, J., Ben-Soussàn, T. D., & Goldstein, A. (2017). Creativity is enhanced by long-term mindfulness training and is negatively correlated with trait default-mode-related low-gamma inter-hemispheric connectivity. *Mindfulness, 8*(3), 717–727. https://doi.org/10.1007/s12671-016-0649-y

Beyer, S. V. (2016). *Talking stick: Peacemaking as a spiritual path.* New York, NY: Simon & Schuster.

Blakey, J. D. (2015). *The impact of workspace on innovation* (Doctoral dissertation). Retrieved from ProQuest Dissertations and Theses (UMI No: 3702901).

Boucher, R. H. (2014). *Creative breakthrough emergence: A conversational accomplishment* (Doctoral dissertation). Retrieved from ProQuest Dissertations and Theses (UMI No: 3642065).

Boyce, B. (Ed.). (2011). *The mindfulness revolution: Leading psychologists, scientists, artists, and meditation teachers on the power of mindfulness in everyday life.* Boulder, CO: Shambhala Publications.

Brown, B. (2018). *Dare to lead: Brave work, tough conversations, whole hearts.* London, UK: Vermillion.

Brown, J. (2002). *The world café: Living knowledge through conversations that matter* (Doctoral dissertation). Retrieved from ProQuest Dissertations and Theses (UMI No: 3041666).

Brown, J., & Isaacs, D. (2005). *The world café: Shaping our futures through conversations that matter.* San Francisco, CA: Berrett-Koehler Publishers, Inc.

Burkus, D. (2013). *Myths of creativity: The truth about how innovative companies and people generate great ideas.* Somerset, NJ: John Wiley & Sons, Inc.

Byrne, E. K. (2017). *Mindful creativity: An exploration of a mindfulness intervention on workgroup creativity* (Doctoral dissertation). Retrieved from ProQuest Dissertations and Theses (UMI No: 10271540).

Capurso, V., Fabbro, F., & Crescentini, C. (2014). Mindful creativity: The influence of mindfulness meditation on creative thinking. *Frontiers in Psychology, 4.* Article 1020. https://doi.org/10.3389/fpsyg.2013.01020

Car, M., Kanjuo-Mrcela, A., & Mesner-Andolsek, D. (2015). Artful making: Use of principles of artistic creation in management. *Teorija in Praksa, 52*(3), 511–537.

Carroll, M. (2010, March). Beyond the elevator speech. *Shambhala Sun,* pp. 54–57.

Carroll, M. (2011). At work, don't be a know-it-all. In B. Boyce (Ed.), *The mindfulness revolution: Leading psychologists, scientists, artists, and meditation teachers on the power of mindfulness in daily life* (pp. 97–100). Boulder, CO: Shambhala Publications.

Chesshire, C. (2009). *The illustrated encyclopedia of Japanese gardening.* London, UK: Hermes House.

Chödrön, P. (1991). *The wisdom of no escape and the path of loving-kindness.* Boston, MA: Shambhala Publications.

Chödrön, P. (2001). *The places that scare you: A guide to fearlessness in difficult times.* Boston, MA: Shambhala Publications.

Chödrön, P. (2013). *How to meditate: A practical guide to making friends with your mind.* Lewisville, CO: Sounds True.

Cleirigh, D. O., & Greaney, J. (2014). Mindfulness and group performance: An exploratory investigation into the effects of brief mindfulness intervention on group task performance. *Mindfulness, 6,* 601–609.

Colzato, L. S., Ozturk, A., & Hommel, B. (2012). Meditate to create: The impact of focused-attention and open-monitoring training on convergent and divergent thinking. *Frontiers in Psychology, 3,* 116. https://doi.org/10.3389/fpsyg.2012.00116

Contemplative Art. (2000–2015). Retrieved from https://www.contemplativemind.org/practices/tree/contemplativeart

Conti, R., & Amabile, T. M. (2011). Motivation. In M. A. Runco & S. R. Pritzker (Eds.), *Encyclopedia of creativity* (Vol. 1, 2nd ed., pp. 147–152). San Diego, CA: Academic Press.

Crescentini, C., & Capurso, V. (2015). Mindfulness meditation and explicit and implicit indicators of personality and self-concept changes. *Frontiers in Psychology, 6*(44). https://doi.org/10.3389/fpsyg.2015.00044

Csikszentmihalyi, M. (1990). *Flow: The psychology of optimal experience.* New York, NY: HarperCollins.

Csikszentmihalyi, M. (1996/2013). *Creativity: The psychology of discovery and invention.* New York, NY: HarperCollins.

Csikszentmihalyi, M. (1999). Implications of a systems perspective for the study of creativity. In R. J. Sternberg (Ed.), *Handbook of creativity* (pp. 313–335). New York, NY: Cambridge University Press.

Daido Loori, J. (2004). *The Zen of creativity: Cultivating your artistic life.* New York, NY: Ballantine Books.

Damasio, A. (1999). *The feeling of what happens: Body and emotion in the making of consciousness.* New York, NY: Houghton Mifflin Harcourt.

Damasio, A. (2010). *Self comes to mind: Constructing the conscious brain.* New York, NY: Vintage Books.

Davis, D. M., & Hayes, J. A. (2011). What are the benefits of mindfulness? A practice review of psychotherapy-related research. *Psychotherapy, 48*(2), 198–208. https://doi.org/10.1037/a0022062

De Dreu, C. K. W., Baas, M., & Nijstad, B. A. (2012). The emotive roots of creativity: Basic and applied issues on affect and motivation. In M. Mumford (Ed.), *Handbook of organizational creativity* (pp. 217–240). San Diego, CA: Academic Press.

Dhiman, S. (2017). *Holistic leadership: A new paradigm for today's leaders.* New York, NY: Palgrave Macmillan.

Donohue, K. T. (2011). Expressive arts therapy. In M. Runco & S. Pritzker (Eds.), *Encyclopedia of creativity* (Vol. 1, 2nd ed., pp. 497–501). San Diego, CA: Academic Press.

Dreyfus, H. L. (2006). The current relevance of Merleau-Ponty's phenomenology of embodiment. *The Electronic Journal of Analytic Philosophy, 4.* Retrieved from http://ejap.louisiana.edu/ejap/1996.spring/dreyfus.1996.spring.html

Duhigg, C. (2016, February 25). What Google learned from its quest to build a perfect team. *The New York Times Magazine.* Retrieved from www.nytimes.com/2016/02/28/magazine/what-google-learned-from-its-quest-to-build-the-perfect-team.html

Edmondson, A. C. (2004). Psychological safety, trust, and learning in organizations: A group-level lens. In R. M. Kramer & K. S. Cook (Eds.), *Trust and distrust in organizations: Dilemmas and approaches* (pp. 239–272). New York, NY: Russell Sage Foundation.

Edmondson, A. C. (2019). *The fearless organization: Creating psychological safety in the workplace for learning, innovation, and growth.* Hoboken, NJ: John Wiley & Sons, Inc.

Ejamabo, N. O. (2015). The influence of decision making in organizational leadership and management activities. *Journal of Entrepreneurship and Organization Management, 4*(2). https://doi.org/10.4172/2169-026X.1000138

Erlich, J. (2015). Creating mindful leaders and organizations. *People + Strategy, 38*(3), 22–25.

Fogel, A. (2009). *Body sense: The science and practice of embodied self-awareness.* New York, NY: Norton.

Freeman, R. (2017). *The talking stick way: An indigenous research methodology for engaging diverse global conversations* (Master's thesis). Retrieved from https://shareok.org/handle/11244/52926

Gelb, D. (Director). (2017, February 17). Jeong Kwan [Television series episode]. In A. Fried & D. Gelb (Executive producers), *Chef's table* (Season 3, Episode 1). Los Gatos, CA: Netflix.

Gendlin, E. T. (1978). *Focusing.* New York, NY: Random House.

George, J. (2007). Creativity in organizations. *The Academy of Management Annals, 1*(1), 439–477. https://doi.org/10.1080/078559814

Giles, H., Denes, A., Hamilton, D. L., & Hajda, J. M. (2009). Striking a chord: A prelude to music and intergroup relations research. *Group Processes & Intergroup Relations, 12*(3), 291–301.

Gillam, T. (2018). *Creativity, wellbeing and mental health practice.* London, UK: Palgrave Macmillan.

Goldberg, N. (1986). *Writing down the bones.* Boston, MA: Shambhala Publications.

Goleman, D. (1995/2005). *Emotional intelligence: Why it can matter more than IQ* (10th anniversary ed.). New York, NY: Bantam Books.

Goleman, D. (2011). *Leadership: The power of emotional intelligence.* Florence, MA: More Than Sound.

Goleman, D., & Lippincott, M. (2017). Without emotional intelligence, mindfulness doesn't work. *Harvard Business Review.* Retrieved from https://hbr.org/2017/09/sgc-what-really-makes-mindfulness-work

Gondo, E. (2018, September 20). *5 authentic relating techniques that dissolve tension in the workplace.* Conscious Company. Retrieved from https://consciouscompanymedia.com/workplace-culture/authentic-relating-workplace/

Good, D. J., Lyddy, C. J., Glomb, T. M., Bono, J. E., Brown, K. W., Duffy, M. K., … Lazar, S. W. (2016). Contemplating mindfulness at work: An integrative review. *Journal of Management, 42*(1), 114–142. https://doi.org/10.1177/0149206315617003

Goslin-Jones, T. (2010). *The perceived effects of person-centered expressive arts on one's work experience* (Doctoral dissertation). Retrieved from ProQuest Dissertations and Theses (UMI No: 3418296).

Goslin-Jones, T. (2011). Using expressive arts to transform the workplace. In N. Rogers (Ed.), *The creative connection for groups: Person-centered expressive arts for healing and social change* (pp. 354–357). Palo Alto, CA: Science and Behavior Books.

Goslin-Jones, T., & Herron, S. (2016). Cutting edge person-centered expressive arts. In C. Lago & D. Charr (Eds.), *The person-centered counseling and psychotherapy handbook* (pp. 199–211). New York, NY: Open University Press, McGraw-Hill Education.

Groysberg, B., Lee, J., Price, J., & Cheng, Y. (2018, January–February). The leader's guide to corporate culture. *Harvard Business Review*. Retrieved from https://hbr.org/2018/01/the-culture-factor

Guilford, J. P. (1967). Creativity: Yesterday, today and tomorrow. *The Journal of Creative Behavior, 1*(1), 3–14. https://doi.org/10.1002/j.2162-6057.1967.tb00002.x

Haidt, J. (2006). *The happiness hypothesis: Finding modern truth in ancient wisdom.* New York, NY: Basic Books.

Halprin, D. (2003). *The expressive body in life, art and therapy: Working with movement, metaphor and meaning.* Philadelphia, PA: Jessica Kingsley Publishers.

Hanson, R. (2015, March 16). *What is mindful presence?* Retrieved from https://www.rickhanson.net/mindful-presence-2/

Hargadon, A. B., & Bechky, B. A. (2006). When collections of creatives become creative collectives: A field study of problem solving at work. *Organization Science, 17*(4), 484–500.

Hart, S. (2008). *Brain, attachment, personality: An introduction to neuro-affective development.* London, UK: Karnac.

Harvey, S. (1994). Dynamic play therapy: An integrated expressive arts approach to the family treatment of infants and toddlers. *Zero to Three, 15*(1), 11–18.

Hawkins, P., & Smith, N. (2014). Transformational coaching. In E. Cox, T. Bachkirova, & D. A. Clutterbuck (Eds.), *The complete handbook of coaching* (pp. 228–243). Thousand Oaks, CA: Sage.

Hess von Ludewig, H. K. (2014). *Networked creativity: Understanding the process and effect of interpersonal and networked interactions on workplace creativity* (Doctoral dissertation). Retrieved from ProQuest Dissertations and Theses (UMI No: 3647627).

Hayashi, A. (2017). *Social presencing theater.* Retrieved from https://arawana-hayashi.com

Holden, J., & Hewison, R. (2011). *Cultural leadership handbook: How to run a creative organization.* Farnham, UK: Ashgate Publishing Group.

Holm, M. (2014). Cultivating alternate mindsets to restructure the global economy by reducing stress and enhancing innovation. *The Business and Management Review, 5*(1), 279–289.

Hyland, P. K., Lee, R. A., & Mills, M. J. (2015). Mindfulness at work: A new approach to improving individual and organizational performance. *Industrial and Organizational Psychology, 8*(4), 576–602. https://doi.org/10.1017/iop.2015.41

Ivcevic, Z., Moeller, J., Menges, J., & Brackett, M. (2020). Supervisor emotionally intelligent behavior and employee creativity. *Journal of Creative Behavior*. https://doi.org/10.1002/jocb.436

James, K., & Drown, D. (2012). Organizations and creativity: Trends in research, status of education and practice, agenda for the future. In M. Mumford (Ed.), *Handbook of organizational creativity* (pp. 17–38). San Diego, CA: Academic Press.

Janson, H. W. (1986). *History of art* (3rd ed.). New York, NY: Harry N. Abrams.

John-Steiner, V. (2000). *Creative collaboration*. New York, NY: Oxford University Press.

John-Steiner, V. (2011). Collaboration. In M. Runco & S. Pritzker (Eds.), *Encyclopedia of creativity* (2nd ed., pp. 222–225). San Diego, CA: Academic Press.

Joo, B., McLean, G. N., & Yang, B. (2013). Creativity and human resource development: An integrative literature review and a conceptual framework for future research. *Human Resource Development Review, 12*(4), 390–421.

Kabat-Zinn, J. (1991). *Full catastrophe living: Using the wisdom of your body and mind to face stress, pain, and illness*. New York, NY: Delta Trade Paperbacks.

Kabat-Zinn, J. (1994). *Wherever you go, there you are: Mindfulness meditation in everyday life*. New York, NY: Hyperion Books.

Kafka, F. (1973). *Shorter works of Franz Kafka* (M. Paisley, Ed. and Trans.). London, UK: Secker & Warburg.

Karr, A., & Wood, M. (2011). *The practice of contemplative photography: Seeing the world with fresh eyes*. Boston, MA: Shambhala Publications.

Kaufman, J. C., & Beghetto, R. A. (2009). Beyond big and little: The four C model of creativity. *Review of General Psychology, 13*(1), 1–12. https://doi.org/10.1037/a0013688

Kaufman, S. B. (2013). Opening up openness to experience: A four-factor model and relations to creative achievement in the arts and sciences. *The Journal of Creative Behavior, 47*(4), 233–255. https://doi.org/10.1002/jocb.33

Kaufman, S. B., & Gregoire, C. (2015). *Wired to create: Unraveling the mysteries of the creative mind*. New York, NY: Perigee.

Kaufman, S. B., Quilty, L. C., Grazioplene, R. G., Hirsh, J. B., Gray, J. R., Peterson, J. B., & DeYoung, C. G. (2016). Openness to experience and intellect differentially predict creative achievement in the arts and sciences. *Journal of Personality, 84*(2), 248–258. https://doi.org/10.1111/jopy.12156

Kaviani, H., & Hatami, N. (2016). Link between mindfulness and personality-related factors including empathy, theory of mind, openness, pro-social behaviour and suggestibility. *Clinical Depression, 2*, 119. https://doi.org/10.4172/2572-0791.1000119

Kleiner, A. (2017, August 7). What the body tells us about leadership. *Strategy + Business.* Retrieved from https://www.strategy-business.com/article/What-the-Body-Tells-Us-about-Leadership?gko=f5217

Koller, J. M., & Koller, P. (1991). *A sourcebook in Asian philosophy.* Upper Saddle River, NJ: Prentice Hall.

Koren, L. (1994). *Wabi sabi for artists, designers, poets and philosophers.* Berkeley, CA: Stone Bridge Press.

Kornfield, J. (2008). *The wise heart: A guide to the universal teachings of Buddhist psychology.* New York, NY: Bantam Books.

Kozbelt, A., Beghetto, R. A., & Runco, M. A. (2010). Theories of creativity. In J. C. Kaufman & R. J. Sternberg (Eds.), *The Cambridge handbook of creativity* (pp. 20–47). New York, NY: Cambridge University Press.

Kudesia, R. S. (2015). Mindfulness and creativity in the workplace. In J. Reb & P. Atkins (Eds.), *Mindfulness in organizations: Foundations, research, and applications* (Cambridge Companions to Management) (pp. 190–212). Cambridge: Cambridge University Press. https://doi.org/10.1017/CBO9781107587793.010

Langer, E. (1989/2014). *Mindfulness* (25th anniversary ed.). Boston, MA: Da Capo Press.

Langer, E. (2005). *On becoming an artist—Reinventing yourself through mindful creativity.* New York, NY: Ballantine Books.

Langer, E. (2014, March). Mindfulness in the age of complexity. *Harvard Business Review*, pp. 68–73. Retrieved from https://hbr.org/2014/03/mindfulness-in-the-age-of-complexity

"Leadership." (2019). Retrieved December 26, 2019, from O.C. Tanner Global Culture Report website: https://www.octanner.com/global-culture-report/2020/leadership.html

Lebuda, I., Zabelina, D. L., & Karwowski, M. (2016). Mind full of ideas: A meta-analysis of the mindfulness–creativity link. *Personality and Individual Differences, 93*, 22–26. https://doi.org/10.1016/j.paid.2015.09.040

Lee, G., & Roberts, I. (2010). Coaching for authentic leadership. In J. Passmore (Ed.), *Leadership coaching: Working with leaders to develop elite performance* (pp. 17–34). London, UK: Kogan Page.

Leonard, K., & Yorton, T. (2015). *Yes, And: How improvisation reverses "No, But" thinking and improves creativity and collaboration—Lessons from the Second City.* New York, NY: HarperCollins.

Levine, E. G., & Levine, S. K. (Eds.). (2011). *Art in action: Expressive arts therapy and social change*. Philadelphia, PA: Jessica Kingsley Publishers.

Levine, S. K., & Levine, E. (Eds.). (1999). *Foundations of expressive arts therapy: Theoretical and clinical perspectives*. London, UK: J. Kingsley Publishers.

Marion, R. (2012). Leadership of creativity: Entity-based, relational, and complexity perspectives. In M. Mumford (Ed.), *Handbook of organizational creativity* (pp. 457–479). San Diego, CA: Academic Press.

Marlow, S. L., Lacerenza, C. N., Woods, A. L., & Salas, E. (2018). Training creativity in teams. In R. Reiter-Palmon (Ed.), *Team creativity and innovation* (pp. 283–306). New York, NY: Oxford University Press.

Marturano, J. (2013, August 5). What is a 'mindful leader?'. [Web log post]. Retrieved from https://instituteformindfulleadership.org/mindful-leader/

Maslow, A. (1962/2011). *Toward a psychology of being*. Mansfield Centre, CT: Martino Publishing.

May, R. (1975). *The courage to create*. New York, NY: W. W. Norton & Co.

McGarry, L. M., & Russo, F. A. (2011). Mirroring in dance/movement therapy: Potential mechanisms behind empathy enhancement. *The Arts in Psychotherapy, 38*(3), 178–184.

McQuade, J., & Hall, M. (2015). *Looking and seeing: Nalanda Miksang contemplative photography*. Madison, WI: Drala Publishing.

Merleau-Ponty, M. (1948/2004). *The world of perception* (O. Davis, Trans.). New York, NY: Routledge.

Merleau-Ponty, M. (1964). Eye and mind. In J. E. Edie (Ed.), *The primacy of perception* (C. Dallery, Trans., pp. 159–190). Evanston, IL: Northwestern University Press.

Milliken, F. J., Bartel, C. A., & Kurtzberg, T. R. (2003). Diversity and creativity in work groups: A dynamic perspective on the affective and cognitive processes that link diversity and performance. In P. B. Paulus & B. A. Nijstad (Eds.), *Group creativity: Innovation through collaboration* (pp. 32–62). New York, NY: Oxford University Press.

Mirza, B. (2019, September 25). Toxic workplace cultures hurt workers and company profits. [Web log post]. Retrieved from https://www.shrm.org/resourcesandtools/hr-topics/employee-relations/pages/toxic-workplace-culture-report.aspx

Miyashiro, M. R. (2011). *The empathy factor: Your competitive advantage for personal, team, and business success*. Encinitas, CA: Puddle Jumper Press.

Moultrie, J., Nilsson, M., Dissel, M., Haner, U. E., Janssen, S., & Van der Lugt, R. (2007). Innovation spaces: Towards a framework for understanding the role of the physical environment in innovation. *Creativity and Innovation Management, 16*(1), 53–65.

Müller, B. C. N., Gerasimova, A., & Ritter, S. M. (2016). Concentrative meditation influences creativity by increasing cognitive flexibility. *Psychology of*

Aesthetics, Creativity, and the Arts, 10(3), 278–286. https://doi.org/10.1037/a0040335

Mumford, M. D., Hester, K. S., & Robledo, I. C. (2012). Creativity in organizations: Importance and approaches. In M. Mumford (Ed.), *Handbook of organizational creativity* (pp. 3–16). San Diego, CA: Academic Press.

Mumford, M. D., Mulhearn, T. J., Watts, L. L., Steele, L. M., & McIntosh, T. (2018). Leader impacts on creative teams: Direction, engagement, and sales. In R. Reiter-Palmon (Ed.), *Team creativity and innovation* (pp. 131–166). New York, NY: Oxford University Press.

Mumford, M. D., & Todd, E. M. (Eds.). (2020). *Creativity and innovation in organizations*. New York, NY: Routledge.

Mumford, M. D., Todd, E. M., Higgs, C., & Martin, R. (2020). What is needed to think creatively at work? Knowledge and skills. In M. D. Mumford & E. M. Todd (Eds.), *Creativity and innovation in organizations*. New York, NY: Routledge. Retrieved from https://books.google.com/books?id=30i8DwAAQBAJ&lpg=PT6&pg=PT70#v=onepage&q&f=false

Nemeth, C. J., & Nemeth-Brown, B. (2003). Better than individuals? The potential benefits of dissent and diversity for group creativity. In P. B. Paulus & B. A. Nijstad (Eds.), *Group creativity: Innovation through collaboration* (pp. 63–84). New York, NY: Oxford University Press.

Nemeth, C. J., & O'Connor, A. (2019). Better than individuals?: Dissent and group creativity. In P. B. Paulus & B. A. Nijstad (Eds.), *The Oxford handbook of group creativity and innovation* (pp. 73–83). Oxford, UK: Oxford University Press.

Oades-Sese, G. V., & Esquivel, G. B. (2011). Cultural diversity and creativity. In M. A. Runco & S. R. Pritzker (Eds.), *Encyclopedia of creativity* (Vol. 1, 2nd ed., pp. 335–341). San Diego, CA: Academic Press.

O'Brien, K. (2016, December 9). Listening as activism: The "Sonic meditations" of Pauline Oliveros. *The New Yorker*. Retrieved from https://www.newyorker.com/culture/culture-desk/listening-as-activism-the-sonic-meditations-of-pauline-oliveros

Okuda, S., Runco, M., & Berger, D. (1991). Creativity and the finding and solving of real-world problems. *Journal of Psychoeducational Assessment, 9*(1), 45–53.

Olendzki, A. (2010). *Unlimiting mind: The radically experiential psychology of Buddhism*. Boston, MA: Wisdom Publications.

Oliveros, P. (1974). *Sonic meditations*. Baltimore, MD: Smith Publications.

Osborne, W. (2000). *Sounding the abyss of otherness: Pauline Oliveros' deep listening and the sonic meditations* (originally published as Chap. 3 of *Women making art*). Retrieved from http://www.osborne-conant.org/oliveros.htm

Oshry, B. (2010). Coaching from a systems perspective. In J. Passmore (Ed.), *Leadership coaching: Working with leaders to develop elite performance* (pp. 187–209). London, UK: Kogan Page.

Pater, P. (2013, September). The art of creative, high-performance leadership. *Professional Safety*, pp. 37–40.

Paulus, P. B., & Brown, V. R. (2003). Enhancing ideational creativity in groups: Lessons from research on brainstorming. In P. B. Paulus & B. A. Nijstad (Eds.), *Group creativity: Innovation through collaboration* (pp. 110–136). New York, NY: Oxford University Press.

Paulus, P. B., Dzindolet, M., & Kohn, N. W. (2012). Collaborative creativity—Group creativity and team innovation. In M. Mumford (Ed.), *Handbook of organizational creativity* (pp. 327–357). London, UK: Academic Press.

Paulus, P. B., & Kenworthy, J. B. (2019). Effective brainstorming. In P. B. Paulus & B. A. Nijstad (Eds.), *The Oxford handbook of group creativity and innovation* (pp. 287–306). Oxford, UK: Oxford University Press.

Pickert, K. (2014, January 23). The mindful revolution. *Time Magazine*. Retrieved from http://time.com/1556/the-mindful-revolution/

Pirson, M., Langer, E. J., Bodner, T., & Zilcha-Mano, S. (2012, October 8). The development and validation of the Langer mindfulness scale—Enabling a socio-cognitive perspective of mindfulness in organizational contexts. New York, NY: Fordham University School of Business Research Paper. https://doi.org/10.2139/ssrn.2158921

Plucker, J. A., & Makel, M. C. (2010). Assessment of creativity. In J. C. Kaufman & R. J. Sternberg (Eds.), *The Cambridge handbook of creativity* (pp. 48–73). New York, NY: Cambridge University Press.

Pritzker, S. (2011). Zen. In M. A. Runco & S. R. Pritzker (Eds.), *Encyclopedia of creativity* (Vol. 2, 2nd ed., pp. 539–543). San Diego, CA: Academic Press.

Proust, M. (1923). *La Prisonniere*. Quote retrieved from https://www.goodreads.com/quotes/33702-the-real-voyage of discovery-consists-not-in-seeking-new

Pruetipibultham, O., & McLean, G. N. (2010). The role of arts in organizational settings. *Human Resource Development Review, 9*(1), 3–25.

Raskin, J. D. (2012). Evolutionary constructivism and humanistic psychology. *Journal of Theoretical and Philosophical Psychology, 32*, 119–133.

Reiter-Palmon, R. (Ed.). (2018). *Team creativity and innovation*. New York, NY: Oxford University Press.

Reiter-Palmon, R., Wigert, B., & de Vreede, T. (2012). Team creativity and innovation: The effect of group composition, social processes, and cognition. In M. D. Mumford (Ed.), *Handbook of organizational creativity* (pp. 295–326). Cambridge, UK: Academic Press.

Richards, R. (Ed.). (2007). *Everyday creativity and new views of human nature: Psychological, social, and spiritual perspectives*. Washington, DC: American Psychological Association.

Richards, R. (2010). Everyday creativity: Process and way of life—Four key issues. In J. C. Kaufman & R. J. Sternberg (Eds.), *The Cambridge handbook of creativity* (pp. 189–215). New York, NY: Cambridge University Press.

Richards, R. (2018). *Everyday creativity and the healthy mind: Dynamic new paths for self and society*. London, UK: Palgrave Macmillan.

Rietzschel, E. F., Nijstad, B. A., & Stroebe, W. (2019). Why great ideas are often overlooked: A review and theoretical analysis of research on idea selection and evaluation. In P. B. Paulus & B. A. Nijstad (Eds.), *The Oxford handbook of group creativity and innovation* (pp. 179–196). Oxford, UK: Oxford University Press.

Rogers, C. (1961). *On becoming a person: A therapist's view of psychotherapy*. New York, NY: Houghton Mifflin Company.

Rogers, N. (1993). *The creative connection: Expressive arts as healing*. Palo Alto, CA: Science & Behavior Books, Inc.

Rogers, N. (2011). *The creative connection for groups: Person-centered expressive arts for healing and social change*. Palo Alto, CA: Science & Behavior Books, Inc.

Romanyshyn, R. D. (2012). The necessity for the humanities in psychology: The psychologist and his/her shadow. *The Humanistic Psychologist, 40*, 234–245. https://doi.org/10.1080/08873267.2012.696504

Rosenberg, M. B. (2003). *Nonviolent communication: A language of life*. Encinitas, CA: PuddleDancer Press.

Rothouse, M. (2018). *Facilitating team creativity and collaboration using mindfulness and contemplative arts* (Doctoral dissertation). Retrieved from ProQuest Dissertations and Theses (Order No. 10823776).

Rozovsky, J. (2015, November 17). The five keys to a successful Google team. Retrieved from https://rework.withgoogle.com/blog/five-keys-to-a-successful-google-team/

Runco, M. A. (Ed.). (1994). *Problem finding, problem solving, and creativity*. Norwood, NJ: Ablex.

Rupprecht, S., Falke, P., Kohls, N., Tamdjidi, C., Wittmann, M., & Kersemaekers, W. (2019). Mindful leader development: How leaders experience the effects of mindfulness training on leader capabilities. *Frontiers in Psychology, 10*, 1081. https://doi.org/10.3389/fpsyg.2019.01081

Saitzyk, S. (2013). *Place your thoughts here: Meditation for the creative mind*. Los Angeles, CA: First Thought Press.

Sand, K. S. (2015). *Fostering creativity: Adopting mindfulness as an innovative approach* (Doctoral dissertation). Retrieved from ProQuest Dissertations and Theses (Accession Order No. 3717293).

Sartwell, C. (2012). Beauty. In *Stanford Encyclopedia of Philosophy*. Retrieved from http://plato.stanford.edu/entries/beauty/

Sawyer, K. (2017). *Group genius: The creative power of collaboration* (2nd ed.). New York, NY: Basic Books.

Sawyer, R. K., & DeZutter, S. (2009). Distributed creativity: How collective creations emerge from collaboration. *Psychology of Aesthetics, Creativity and the Arts, 3*(2), 81–92.

Scharmer, C. O. (2009). *Theory U: Leading from the future as it emerges*. San Francisco, CA: Berrett-Koehler Publishers, Inc.

Scharmer, C. O. (2013, July 9). Uncovering the blind spot of leadership. Retrieved from http://www.dailygood.org/story/450/uncovering-the-blind-spot-of-leadership-c-otto-scharmer/

Scharmer, O. (2018). Leading from the future: A new social technology for our times. Retrieved from https://thesystemsthinker.com/leading-from-the-future-a-new-social-technology-for-our-times/

Schutte, N. S., & Malouff, J. M. (2011). Emotional intelligence mediates the relationship between mindfulness and subjective well-being. *Personality and Individual Differences, 50*(7), 1116–1119.

Schwarz, R. (2015, December). What the research tells us about team creativity and innovation. *Harvard Business Review*. Retrieved from https://hbr.org/2015/12/what-the-research-tells-us-about-team-creativity-and-innovation

Senge, P., Scharmer, O. C., Jaworski, J., & Flowers, B. S. (2004). *Presence: Human purpose and the field of the future*. New York, NY: Crown Business.

Serifsoy, I. (2012). *The leader's muse: An exploration of how artistic sensibilities inform organizational leadership* (Doctoral dissertation). Retrieved from ProQuest Dissertations and Theses (Order No: 3509462).

Shi, B., Dai, D. Y., & Lu, Y. (2016, May). Openness to experience as a moderator of the relationship between intelligence and creative thinking: A study of Chinese children in urban and rural areas. *Frontiers in Psychology, 7*, 641. https://doi.org/10.3389/fpsyg.2016.00641

Siegel, D. (2007). *The mindful brain: Reflection and attunement in the cultivation of well-being*. New York, NY: W. W. Norton & Co.

Siegel, D. (2010). *The mindful therapist: A clinician's guide to mindsight and neural integration*. New York, NY: W. W. Norton & Co.

Siegel, D. (2011). The proven benefits of mindfulness. In B. Boyce (Ed.), *The mindfulness revolution: Leading psychologists, scientists, artists, and meditation teachers on the power of mindfulness in daily life* (pp. 136–139). Boulder, CO: Shambhala Publications.

Siegel, D. (2012). *The developing mind: How relationships and the brain interact to shape who we are*. New York, NY: The Guilford Press.

Siegel, D. (2017). *Mind: A journey to the heart of being human*. New York, NY: W. W. Norton & Co.

Silvia, P. J., Nusbaum, E. C., Berg, C., Martin, C., & O'Connor, A. (2009). Openness to experience, plasticity, and creativity: Exploring lower-order, higher-order, and interactive effects. *Journal of Research in Personality, 43*(6), 1087–1090. https://doi.org/10.1016/j.jrp.2009.04.015

Simonton, D. K. (2012). Fields, domains, and individuals. In M. Mumford (Ed.), *Handbook of organizational creativity* (pp. 67–86). San Diego, CA: Academic Press.

Slater, B. H. (n.d.). Aesthetics. In *Internet Encyclopedia of Philosophy*. Retrieved from http://www.iep.utm.edu/aestheti/

Smith, T. D. (2014). *Using the expressive arts to facilitate group music improvisation and individual reflection: Expanding consciousness in music learning for self-development* (Doctoral dissertation). Retrieved from ProQuest Dissertations and Theses (Order No: 3645985).

Social Presencing Theater: An embodied practice. (2015). Retrieved from https://www.presencing.com/social-presencing-theater

Stasser, G., & Birchmeier, Z. (2003). Group creativity and collective choice. In P. B. Paulus & B. A. Nijstad (Eds.), *Group creativity: Innovation through collaboration* (pp. 85–109). New York, NY: Oxford University Press.

Stedham, Y., & Skaar, T. B. (2019). Mindfulness, trust, and leader effectiveness: A conceptual framework. *Frontiers in Psychology, 10*, 1588. https://doi.org/10.3389/fpsyg.2019.01588

Stromsted, T. (2009). Authentic movement: A dance with the divine. *Body, Movement and Dance in Psychotherapy Journal, 4*, 201–213.

Suckley, L., & Nicholson, J. (2018). Enhancing creativity through workspace design. In L. Martin & N. Wilson (Eds.), *The Palgrave handbook of creativity at work* (pp. 245–263). London, UK: Palgrave Macmillan. https://doi.org/10.1007/978-3-319-77350-6_12

Suzuki, S. (1970/2007). *Zen mind, beginner's mind*. Boston, MA: Weatherhill.

Tan, C. (2012). *Search inside yourself: The unexpected path to achieving success, happiness (and world peace)*. New York, NY: HarperCollins.

Tan, C. (2015, December). Just 6 seconds of mindfulness can make you more effective. *Harvard Business Review*. Retrieved from https://hbr.org/2015/12/just-6-seconds-of-mindfulness-can-make-you-more-effective

Taylor, S. S., & Ladkin, D. (2009). Understanding arts-based methods in managerial development. *Academy of Management Learning & Education, 8*(1), 55–69.

"Teams." (2019). Retrieved December 26, 2019, from O.C. Tanner Global Culture Report website: https://www.octanner.com/global-culture-report/2020/leadership.html

"The Circling™ Method." (2020). Retrieved February 29, 2020, from The Circling Institute website: https://www.circlinginstitute.com/circling/what-is-circling/

Thera, N. (1994). *The foundations of mindfulness: Satipatthana sutta*. Retrieved from http://www.accesstoinsight.org/lib/authors/nyanasatta/wheel019.html

To, M. L., & Fisher, C. D. (2019). Affective influences on creativity in teams: A multilevel regulatory perspective. In P. B. Paulus & B. A. Nijstad (Eds.), *The Oxford handbook of group creativity and innovation* (pp. 103–117). New York, NY: Oxford University Press.

Trungpa, C. (1996/2008). *True perception: The path of dharma art*. Boston, MA: Shambhala Publications.

Van Dam, N. T., van Vugt, M. K., Vago, D. R., Schmalzl, L., Saron, C. D., Olendzki, A., … Meyer, D. E. (2018). Mind the hype: A critical evaluation and prescriptive agenda for research on mindfulness and meditation. *Perspectives on*

Psychological Science, 13(1), 36–61. https://doi.org/10.1177/1745691617709589

Van Ness, D. W., & Strong, K. H. (2014). *Restoring justice: An introduction to restorative justice* (5th ed.). New York, NY: Routledge.

Varela, F. J., Thompson, E., & Rosch, E. (1991). *The embodied mind: Cognitive science and human experience.* Boston, MA: MIT Press.

Vera, D., & Crossan, M. (2005). Improvisation and innovative performance in teams. *Organization Science, 16*(3), 203–224. https://doi.org/10.1287/orsc.1050.0126

Wang, K. (2016). The effect of autonomy on team creativity and the moderating variables. *Journal of Creativity and Business Innovation, 2*, 160–171.

Welwood, J. (2002). *Toward a psychology of awakening: Buddhism, psychotherapy, and the path of personal and spiritual transformation.* Boston, MA: Shambhala Publications.

West, M. A. (1995). Creative values and creative visions in teams at work. In C. M. Ford & D. A. Gioia (Eds.), *Creative action in organizations: Ivory tower visions & real world voices* (pp. 71–77). Thousand Oaks, CA: Sage Publications.

Who we are. (2014). Retrieved from http://ieata.org/who-we-are.html

Whyte, D. (1994/2002). *The heart aroused: Poetry and the preservation of the soul in corporate America.* New York, NY: Crown Business.

Whyte, D. (2001). *Crossing the unknown sea: Work as a pilgrimage of identity.* New York, NY: Riverhead Books.

Whyte, D. (2016, April 6). David Whyte—The conversational nature of reality (K. Tippett, Interviewer). [Audio file]. Retrieved from http://www.onbeing.org/program/david-whyte-the-conversational-nature-of-reality/8560

Zehr, H. (2005). *The little book of contemplative photography: Seeing with wonder, respect, and humility.* Intercourse, PA: Good Books.

Zhou, J., & George, J. M. (2003). Awakening employee creativity: The role of leader in emotional intelligence. *The Leadership Quarterly, 14*(4–5), 545–586.

Zhou, J., & Hoever, I. J. (2014). Research on workplace creativity: A review and redirection. *Annual Review of Organizational Psychology and Organizational Behavior, 1*, 333–359. https://doi.org/10.1146/annurev-orgpsych-031413-091226

Zhou, J., & Shalley, C. E. (2003). Research on employee creativity: A critical review and directions for future research. *Research in Personnel and Human Resources Management, 22*, 165–217. Retrieved from https://psycnet.apa.org/record/2004-12778-004.

Index

M. J. Rothouse, *A Mindful Approach to Team Creativity and Collaboration in Organizations*, Palgrave Studies in Creativity and Innovation in Organizations,
https://doi.org/10.1007/978-3-030-47675-5

The manufacturer's authorised representative in the EU is Springer Nature Customer Service Centre GmbH, Europaplatz 3, 69115 Heidelberg, Germany. If you have any concerns regarding our products, please contact ProductSafety@springernature.com

Printed and bound by CPI Group (UK) Ltd, Croydon, CR0 4YY
25/09/2026
02222903-0004